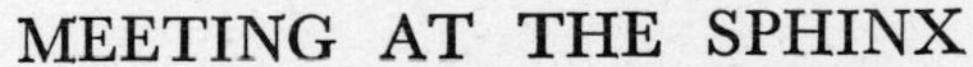

MEETING AT THE SPHINX

BERNARD SHAW AND GABRIEL PASCAL IN SHAW'S STUDY

[*Frontispiece*

MEETING AT THE SPHINX

BY MARJORIE DEANS. GABRIEL PASCAL'S PRODUCTION OF BERNARD SHAW'S

CAESAR AND CLEOPATRA

WITH FOREWORDS BY BOTH THE AUTHOR AND PRODUCER

BERNARD SHAW
AND
GABRIEL PASCAL

MACDONALD & CO (PUBLISHERS) LTD
19 LUDGATE HILL LONDON EC4

MADE AND PRINTED IN GREAT BRITAIN BY PURNELL AND SONS, LTD.,
PAULTON (SOMERSET) AND LONDON

FOREWORD

Gabriel Pascal is one of those extraordinary men who turn up occasionally, say once in a century, and may be called godsends in the arts to which they are devoted. Pascal is doing for the films what Diaghileff did for the Russian Ballet. Until he descended on me out of the clouds I could find nobody who wanted to do anything with my plays on the screen but mutilate them, murder them, give their cadavers to the nearest scrivener, without a notion of how to tell the simplest story in dramatic action, and instructed that there must be a new picture every ten seconds, and that the duration of the whole feature must be forty-five minutes at the extreme outside. The result was to be presented to the public with my name attached, and an assurance that nobody need fear that it had any Shavian quality whatever, and was real genuine Hollywood.

Under such conditions I, of course, would not let my plays be filmed at all, though I quite realized their possibilities in that medium. When Gabriel appeared out of the blue, I just looked at him, and handed him *Pygmalion* to experiment with. His studio was immediately infested with script writers, and he thought that everything they did was wrong and that everything I did was right. Naturally I quite agreed with him. *Pygmalion* was an enormous success. When he tackled *Caesar and Cleopatra* there was not a script writer left in the studio, and when he wanted a new "sequence", he very simply asked me for it and got it.

He shocks me by his utter indifference to the cost; but the result justifies him. The man is a genius: that is all I have to say about him.

G. Bernard Shaw

CREDO

BY GABRIEL PASCAL

I BELIEVE in Miracles! and my strange adventurous life has taught me that there are two kinds of miracle. The first is the so-called Religious Miracle, in which I believe unhesitatingly with all the conviction of my soul. The second is the Miracle of Art. A very intimate relationship exists between these two kinds of miracle; and there is, however strange it may seem to the profane, a religious fervour in the great achievements of art.

From my early youth I struggled to discover my own way to work miracles: whether as a scholarly vagabond; or as a pilgrim follower of Saint Francis; or as a creative artist. I tried the first two ways, and failed. After long wandering and searching, it was my predestination to meet the man who from my boyhood seemed to me to have, since Shakespeare, the greatest God-given gift of expressing the truth through art. This man was G.B.S.

When I met him, we felt instantly that we shared a belief in both kinds of miracle, and that we knew the secret of the Pied Piper—how to induce genuine children to run away from the boring mediocrities of everyday life. So G.B.S. entrusted me with the magic flute of his art, which he knew I could play.

Without that Shavian flute I would have remained only an ordinary vagabond—very funny, maybe; sometimes writing a little song or two to sing on the road to other hobos; but as a creative artist I would have been useless and meaningless. G.B.S. forced me back to my real artistic integrity which many times in life I seemed to have lost. He encouraged me when I doubted myself, and gave me back faith in my spiritual mission. And it became my life work to produce his plays for the screen.

I believe that in time to come the cinema will be the highest form of popular art, because it will include all the arts in itself. Nothing could be more inspiring for me than the unique task of giving evidence to posterity, through my pictures, of the immortality of the genius of Bernard Shaw.

Gabriel Pascal

CONTENTS

LIST OF COLOURED ILLUSTRATIONS

KODACHROMES BY WILFRED NEWTON

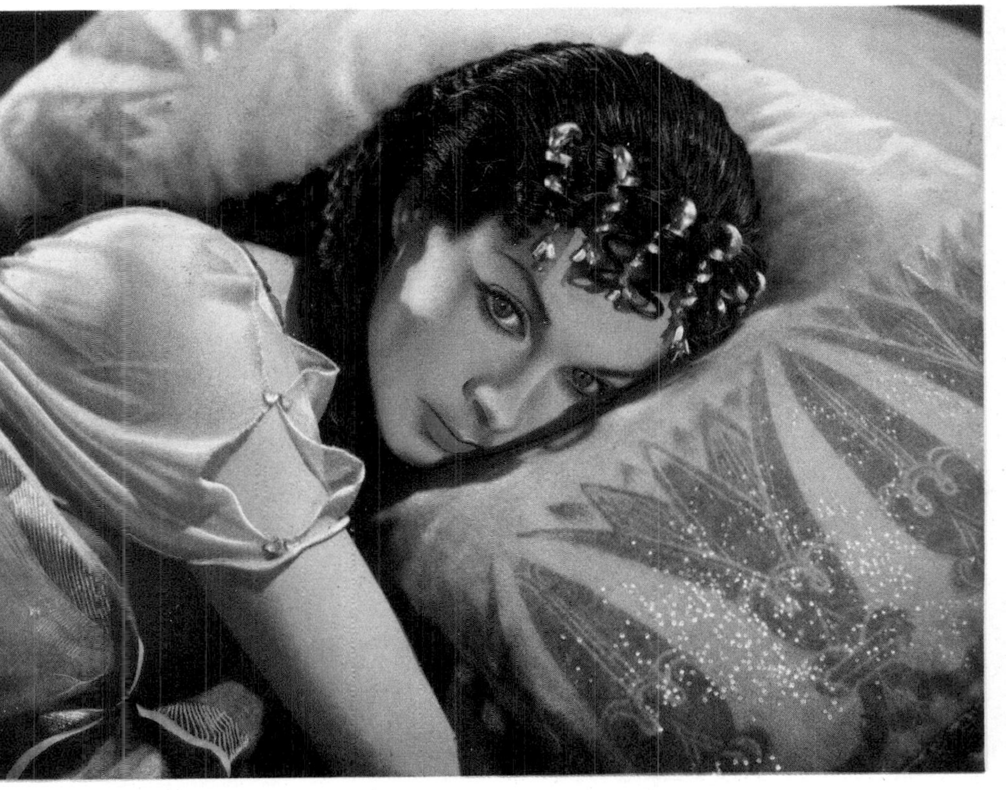

CLEOPATRA AWAKE IN HER BEDROOM IN THE PALACE OF ALEXANDRIA

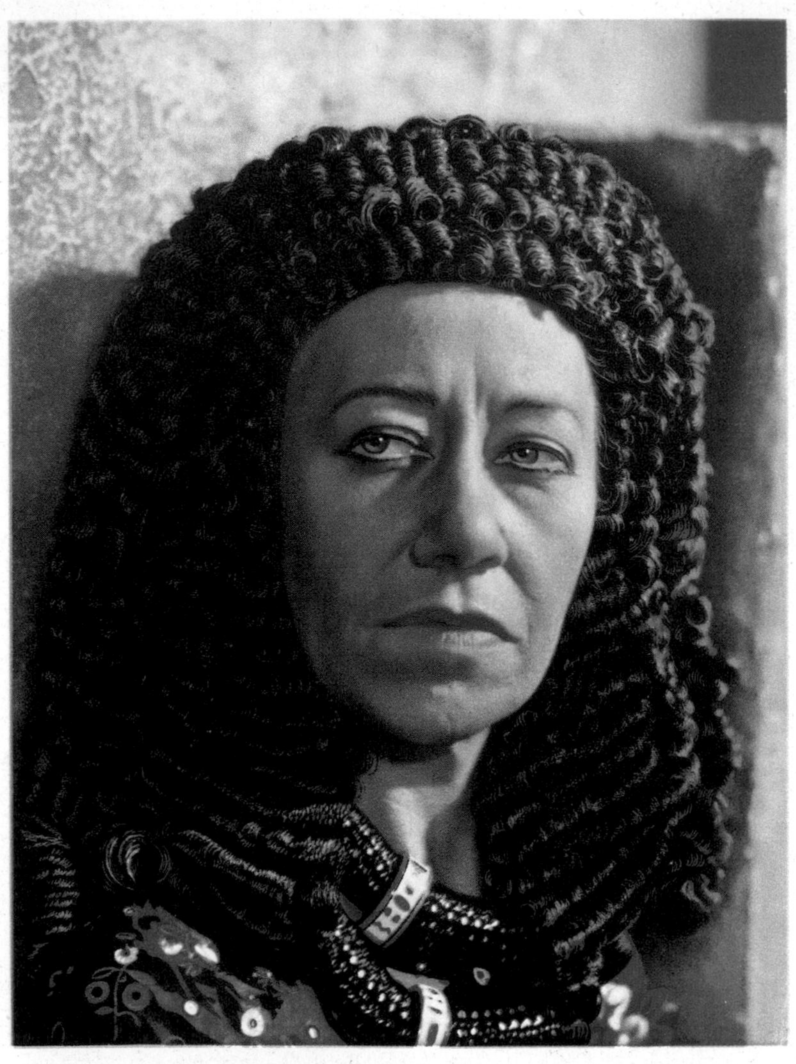

FTATATEETA, NURSE TO CLEOPATRA

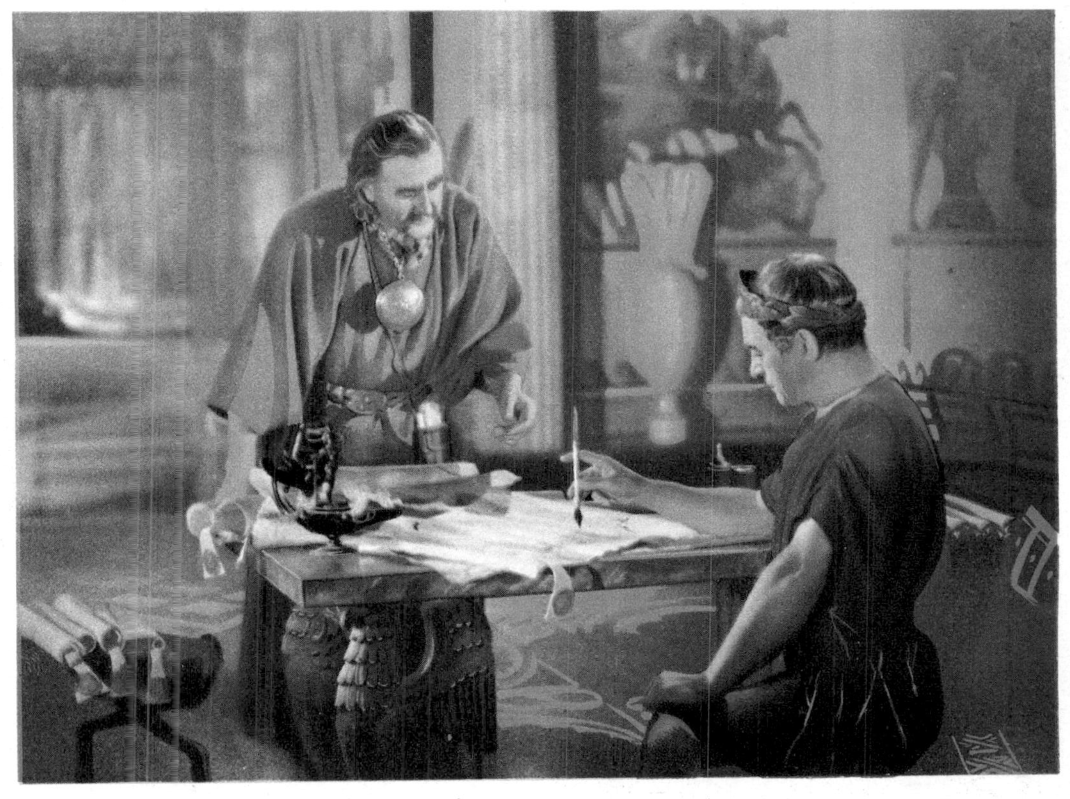

CAESAR GOES OVER HIS PLAN OF CAMPAIGN WITH BRITANNUS

THE CAMEL-MAN LEADS THE HARPIST TO THE PALACE OF ALEXANDRIA

HISTORICAL BACKGROUND

EXTRACT FROM MOMMSEN'S "HISTORY OF ROME"

In Egypt, after the death of Ptolemy Auletes (51 B.C.) his children, Cleopatra about sixteen years of age and Ptolemy Dionysius about ten, had ascended the throne—according to their father's will—jointly, and as consorts; but soon the brother, or rather his guardian Pothinus, had driven the sister from the kingdom and compelled her to seek a refuge in Syria, whence she made preparations to get back to her paternal kingdom. Ptolemy and Pothinus lay with the whole Egyptian army at Pelusium for the sake of protecting the eastern frontier against her, just when Pompey cast anchor at the Casian promontory and sent a request to the king to allow him to land.

The Egyptian court, long informed of the disaster at Pharsalia (*where Caesar had defeated Pompey in battle*), was on the point of rejecting Pompey; but the king's tutor, Theodotus, pointed out that it would be safer, and also preferable with regard to Caesar, if they embraced the opportunity of making away with Pompey. Achillas, the general of the royal troops, and some of Pompey's former soldiers went off in a boat to Pompey's vessel, and invited him to come to the king, and, as the water was shallow, to enter their barge. As he was stepping on the shore, the military tribune, Lucius Septimius, stabbed him from behind (48 B.C.).

When Caesar, following the track of Ptolemy, arrived in the roadstead of Alexandria, all was already over. When the murderer brought to his ship the head of the man who had been his son-in-law and for long years his colleague in rule, and to get whom alive into his power he had come to Egypt, he turned away with deep agitation.

Caesar had now nothing further to do in Egypt, and the Romans and Egyptians expected that he would immediately set sail and apply himself to the huge task of organisation which awaited him after the victory (*of Pharsalia*). But Caesar, faithful to his custom of finally regulating matters at once and in person, wherever he found himself in the wide empire, and firmly convinced that no resistance was to be expected either from the Roman garrison or from the court, being, moreover, in urgent pecuniary embarrassment, landed in Alexandria with the two legions accompanying him, to the number of 3,200 men and 800 Celtic and German cavalry, took up his quarters in the royal palace, and proceeded to collect the necessary sums of money, and to regulate the Egyptian succession, without allowing himself to be disturbed by the saucy remark of Pothinus that Caesar should not for such petty matters neglect his own so important affairs.

In his dealing with the Egyptians he was just and even indulgent. While the arrears of the sum stipulated for in 59 B.C. (*for Roman assistance in an earlier dispute about the throne*) were remitted, there was required merely a final payment of 10,000,000 denarii (£400,000). The belligerent brother and sister were enjoined immediately to suspend hostilities, and were invited to have their dispute investigated and decided by arbitration. They submitted; the royal boy was already in the palace and Cleopatra also presented herself there.[1] Caesar adjudged the kingdom of Egypt to the intermarried brother and sister, Cleopatra and Ptolemy Dionysius.

But a storm was secretly preparing. Alexandria was a cosmopolitan city as well as Rome, hardly inferior to the

[1] Plutarch says:
Caesar privately sent for Cleopatra from her retirement. She took a small boat, and one only of her confidents, Apollodorus, the Sicilian, along with her, and in the dusk of the evening landed near the palace. She was at a loss how to get in undiscovered, till she thought of putting herself into the coverlet of a bed and lying at length, whilst Apollodorus tied up the bedding and carried it on his back through the gates to Caesar's apartment.

Italian capital in the number of its inhabitants, far superior to it in stirring commercial spirit, in skill of handicraft, in taste for science and art. In the citizens there was a lively national self-importance, and a turbulent spirit, which induced them to indulge in their street riots as regularly and as heartily as the Parisians of the present day. One may conceive their feelings when they saw the Roman general ruling in the Palace, and their sovereigns accepting the award of the tribunal. The tumult when the multitude saw the Roman axes carried into the palace, and the numerous assassinations of his soldiers in the city, had taught Caesar the immense danger in which he was placed with his small force in presence of that exasperated multitude. But it was difficult to return on account of the north-west winds prevailing at this season of the year, and the attempt at embarkation might easily become a signal for the outbreak of the insurrection. Besides, it was not Caesar's nature to depart without having accomplished his work.

He accordingly ordered up at once reinforcements from Asia, and, till these arrived, displayed throughout the utmost self-possession. Never was there greater gaiety in his camp than during this rest at Alexandria; and while the beautiful and clever Cleopatra was not sparing of her charms, Caesar also appeared among all his victories to value most those won over beautiful women.

It was a merry prelude to a very grave drama. Under the leadership of Achillas and, as was afterwards proved, by the secret orders of the king and his guardian, the Roman army of occupation stationed in Egypt appeared unexpectedly in Alexandria, and as soon as the citizens saw that it had come to attack Caesar, they made common cause with the soldiers.

With a presence of mind which in some measure justifies his earlier foolhardiness, Caesar hastily collected his scattered men; seized the persons of the king and his minister; entrenched himself in the royal residence and the adjoining theatre; and gave orders, as there was no time to place in safety the war fleet stationed in the principal harbour immediately in front of the theatre, that it should be burnt, and that Pharos, the island with the light-tower commanding the harbour, should be occupied by means of boats. Thus at least a restricted position for defence was secured, and the way was kept open to procure supplies and reinforcements.

The insurrection meanwhile had free course in all Egypt and in the greater part of the capital. As Caesar was not to be overcome from the landward side, the exertions of the besiegers were directed to cut him off from the sea, by which supplies reached him. The island with the lighthouse, and the mole by which this was connected with the mainland, divided the harbour into a western and an eastern half, which were in communication with each other through two arched openings in the mole. Caesar commanded the island and the east harbour, while the mole and the west harbour were in possession of the citizens. Not long afterwards, however, the citizens captured the lighthouse-island and from that point totally closed the narrow and rocky mouth of the east harbour for larger ships; so that Caesar's fleet was compelled to lie in the open roads before the east harbour, and his communication with the sea hung only on a weak thread.

It was absolutely necessary to make an attempt to recover the lighthouse-island. The double attack, which was made by boats from the side of the harbour and by the war vessels from the seaboard, brought not only the island but also the lower part of the mole into Caesar's power; it was only at the second arch-opening of the mole that Caesar ordered the attack to be stopped and the mole to be there closed towards the city by a barricade. But while a violent conflict arose around the entrenchers, the Roman troops left the lower part of the mole adjoining the island bare of defenders: a division of Egyptians landed there unexpectedly, attacked in the rear the

Roman soldiers and sailors crowded together on the mole at the barricade, and drove the whole mass in wild confusion into the sea. A part were taken on board by the Roman ships; the most were drowned. The general himself, who had shared the fate of his men, had been obliged to seek refuge in his ship, and when it sank from having been overloaded with men, he had to save himself by swimming to another.

At length the longed-for relief arrived. Mithridates of Pergamus brought up a motley army by land from Syria. From Pelusium, which he had the fortune to occupy on the day of his arrival, he took the great road towards Memphis. The Egyptians, headed by the young king Ptolemy, whom Caesar had released to his people in the vain hope of allaying the insurrection by this means, despatched an army to the Nile, to detain Mithridates on its further bank. Caesar, on the other hand, as soon as he obtained news of the arrival of the relieving army, conveyed a part of his troops in ships to the end of the Lake of Marea to the west of Alexandria, and marched up this lake and down the Nile, to meet Mithridates advancing up the river.

The junction took place without the enemy attempting to hinder it. Caesar then marched into the Delta, whither the king had retreated, overthrew the Egyptian vanguard at the first onset, and immediately stormed the Egyptian camp itself. The victory was complete; the camp was taken, and those of the Egyptians who did not fall beneath the sword of the enemy were drowned in the attempt to escape to the fleet on the Nile. With one of the boats, which sank overladen with men, the young king also disappeared in the waters of his native stream.

Immediately after the battle, Caesar advanced at the head of his cavalry straight into the portion of the capital occupied by the Egyptians. The enemy received him and sued for peace; and his troops, when they saw him return as victor, welcomed him with boundless joy. The fate of the town lay in Caesar's hands. He exhorted the inhabitants in future earnestly to cultivate the arts of peace alone, and to heal the wounds which they had inflicted on themselves; for the rest, he contented himself with granting to the Jews settled in Alexandria the same rights which the Greek population of the city enjoyed, and with placing in Alexandria, instead of the previous Roman army of occupation, which nominally at least obeyed the king of Egypt, a formal Roman garrison under a commander nominated by himself. For this position of trust a man was purposely selected whose birth made it impossible for him to abuse it—Rufio, an able soldier, but a freedman's son. Cleopatra obtained the sovereignty of Egypt under the supremacy of Rome.

THE STORY

What happens when a famous conqueror, young in heart, but hiding a bald head under the laurel-wreath of his many victories, meets a very young, very beautiful girl who wants to be a Queen?

This is the theme of Bernard Shaw's timeless story, played against a background of starry desert, exquisite Palace interiors humming with gossip and intrigue, and the Mediterranean brilliance of the great Egyptian seaport of Alexandria.

The victorious Roman general, Julius Caesar, comes to Egypt in pursuit of his defeated rival, Pompey. Roaming alone at night in the spacious solitude of the desert, he finds Cleopatra hiding between the paws of the Sphinx, a frightened child running away from the approach of the Roman invaders. She accepts the stranger as a friend, a harmless "old gentleman", and confides in him her terror of the Roman "barbarians", and their legendary leader who lives, so the Egyptians believe, "on human flesh". Caesar is amused and fascinated. He tells Cleopatra that she can save herself from the Roman Monster only by confronting him "as a brave woman and a great queen"; and when, without telling her his name, he reveals the fact that he himself is a Roman, she confidently enlists his help and protection against the dreaded conqueror, and takes him back with her to the ancient desert palace where she is living in exile.

All the courtiers have fled before the rumoured advance of the Romans, and the palace is deserted, save for a

terrified Nubian slave, a couple of cowering girls, and Cleopatra's nurse and familiar tyrant, Ftatateeta, who storms at her for bringing a stranger to the palace without her permission, and for giving orders to the slave in her absence.

Caesar taunts her with her lack of authority, and brings Ftatateeta to her knees with a threat of instant execution at the hands of the slave. Seeing her nurse humbled, Cleopatra snatches up a snakeskin to beat her with and, when she escapes, beats the slave instead, calling out exultantly that she is "a real queen at last, a real, real queen!"

Caesar laughs a little wryly at this sudden change, and tells Cleopatra that she will be "the most dangerous of all Caesar's conquests." But at the mention of this dreaded name, she is again horrified and downcast. She had forgotten Caesar! And now the terrible note of the Roman war-trumpet, the bucina, is heard approaching the Palace. Caesar recalls Ftatateeta, and tells her to prepare the Queen to receive the Roman conqueror.

Assisted by two of the Queen's women, Ftatateeta dresses Cleopatra in her robes of state, and Caesar himself places the crown on her head. The tramp of soldiers' feet is heard outside in the courtyard, the Nubian slave runs panic-stricken through the room, and the waiting-women run after him, screaming. Half-dead with fright, Cleopatra stands on the steps of the throne, waiting for Caesar. And behind her, Caesar himself sits down on the throne, so that when the Roman soldiers march in they come to a halt in front of their general,

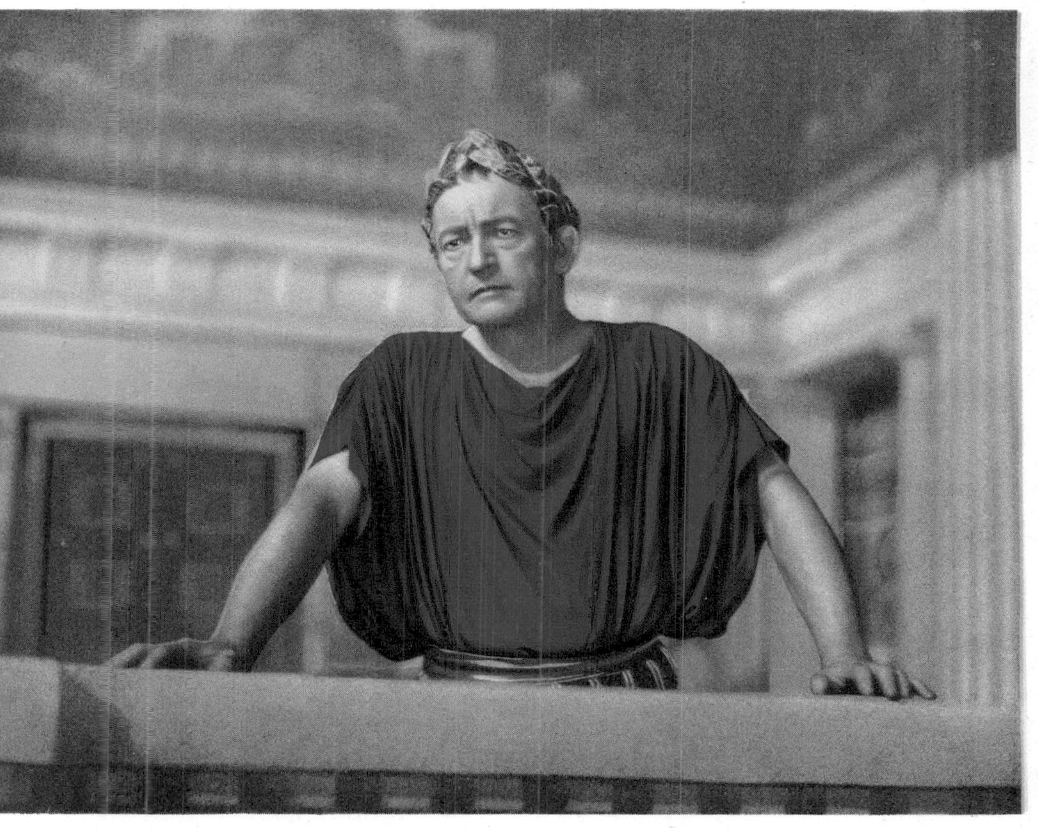

CAESAR ON THE BALCONY OF THE KING'S ROOM

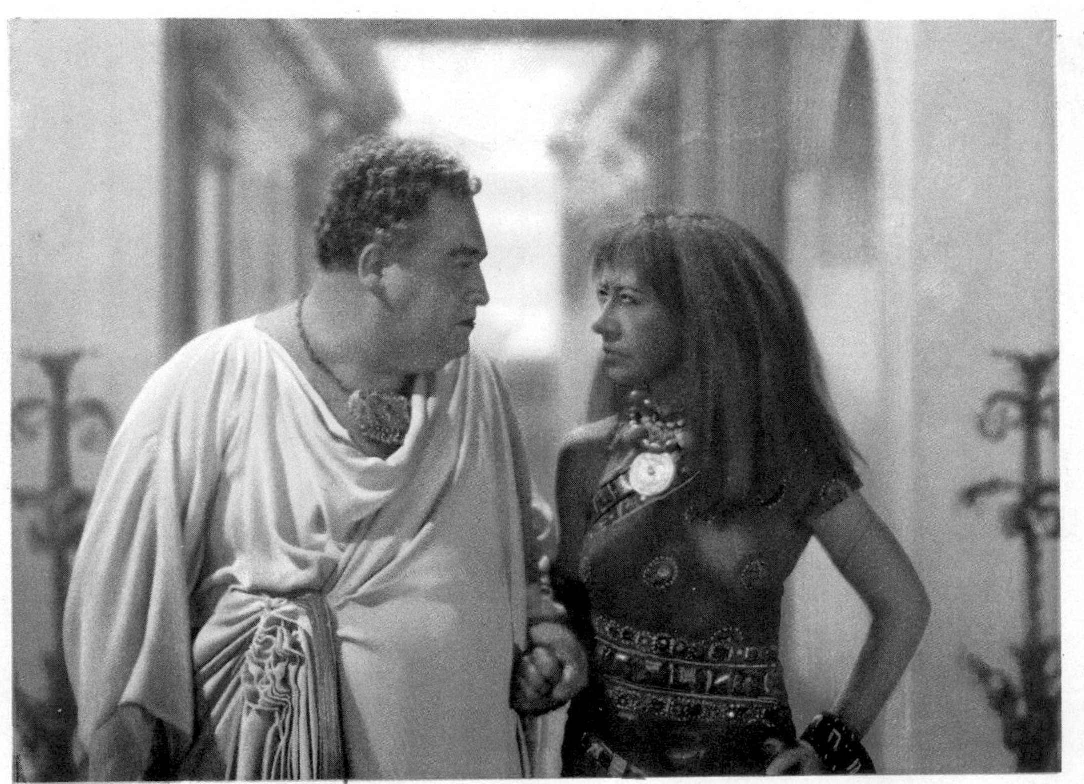

POTHINUS THREATENS FTATATEETA WHEN THEY MEET IN THE PALACE CORRIDOR AT ALEXANDRIA

and salute him with raised swords, shouting: "Hail Caesar!"

Bewildered and incredulous, Cleopatra turns, finds her friend smiling at her, and falls into his arms.

Promising to make Cleopatra the "real" Queen of Egypt, Caesar takes her to Alexandria, where her young brother Ptolemy, supported by a powerful Court faction, occupies the throne. Ptolemy's followers are backed by a standing Roman army, who came to Egypt some years earlier to intervene in a previous dispute about the royal succession, and are now comfortably settled there under the leadership of their general, Achillas. Romans and Egyptians, anxious to uphold their "toy king", Ptolemy, and so keep the power in their own hands, have conspired to curry favour with Caesar by slaying his defeated enemy, Pompey, the moment the latter set foot in Egypt. To their astonishment, Caesar, who makes an unexpected entrance into the Palace Council Chamber with his second-in-command, Rufio, and Britannus, his British-born secretary, condemns their action as cold-blooded murder. He tells them that, while they have been discussing the situation, his troops have surrounded the Palace, and that unless they leave at once he will take the whole lot of them prisoner. Angry and nonplussed, they make their exit, and Cleopatra seats herself delightedly in her brother's place on the throne.

Caesar and Rufio plan to strengthen their position by seizing the Pharos lighthouse and the mole leading to it from the mainland, so making themselves masters of the city harbour; but they are outnumbered and foiled in their strategy by the Egyptian forces. Against Caesar's express orders, Cleopatra has contrived to join him at the Pharos by having herself rolled up in a carpet and carried across the harbour in a boat, rowed by a young Sicilian gallant, Apollodorus; and the whole party only escapes capture by jumping into the sea and swimming to the Roman galleys, Caesar carrying the frightened and bedraggled Queen on his back.

By her own confession afterwards, Cleopatra comes to shore "with much conceit washed out of her". So changed is she, in fact, that her ladies are bored by her new airs of gravity and queenly deportment, as she tries to become the kind of queen Caesar would wish her to be. She has plenty of time to observe his ways, for the failure of the Pharos expedition places the Roman garrison in a dangerous state of siege, and for six months the inmates of the Palace are virtually imprisoned within its walls. Fear of reprisals from Rome makes the superior Egyptian forces reluctant to attack; but Ptolemy's guardian, Pothinus, who is held prisoner by Caesar, tries to stir up trouble between him and Cleopatra by accusing her of treachery to her champion.

Fiercely resentful of the falsity of his charge, which Caesar is inclined to believe, Cleopatra orders Ftatateeta to assassinate Pothinus. The half-savage woman, drunk with blood-lust and revenge on behalf of her young mistress, is delighted to obey. She carries out the order while Cleopatra is entertaining Caesar, with Rufio and Apollodorus, to a banquet on the roof of the Palace; and the feast is interrupted by the death-cry of Pothinus, as he falls into the stone paved courtyard, "with six inches of steel in his ribs". His death enrages the Egyptian mob to the point of attack on the Palace; and it seems that Caesar's cause is lost when, in the nick of time, news is brought to him that the relief has arrived.

Joining forces with the relief army in the desert, Caesar fights and defeats Ptolemy and Achillas. Then, leaving Rufio behind to assist Cleopatra in her task of governing the Egyptians, he sets sail for Rome.

"No tears, dearest Queen," implores the devoted Apollodorus. "He will return some day."

"I hope not," sighs Cleopatra the Queen, ambitious for power; but the child Cleopatra, Caesar's "most dangerous conquest", adds tearfully: "but I can't help crying all the same!"

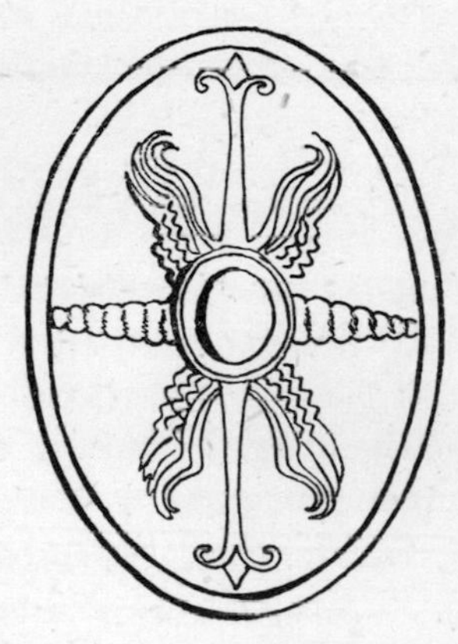

THE SHAW-PASCAL PARTNERSHIP

When Bernard Shaw came to Denham to watch the filming of the meeting between Caesar and Cleopatra on the paws of the Sphinx, he stood for a long time in silence, gazing up at the huge crouching image against its background of starry sky; and his expression, though always critical, reflected also the realization of a fifty-year-old dream.

"What scope! What limitless possibilities!" he said afterwards. "When I look back on my work as a young man with my colleagues in the theatre, it seems to me we were like children playing with wretched makeshift toys. Here you have the whole world to play with!"

To any writer with a real feeling for the drama of humanity, the cinema presents a tremendous lure and challenge. It is inevitable that Bernard Shaw should be fascinated by its opportunities as a dramatic medium—just as surely as Shakespeare would have been, had he lived in our twentieth century instead of in his own.

In the eyes of the world, our claim to fame as a literary nation rests very largely on two, triply alliterative names: Shakespeare and Shaw. Both wrote under the urgent pressure of an age of social change, foreign warfare, the disturbing inrush of new thoughts and alien influences. Both loved—to quote the words of one of them—"the common people". And both of them expressed that love in the same vital, nobly vulgar way, by writing for the stage.

Folk drama, entertainment for the masses—it is no accident that so many of the world's greatest minds should have been turned to the humble catch-penny task of making thousands of ordinary, ignorant people laugh and cry. The drama is essentially a popular art; yet the born dramatic poet must go as far as his genius will carry him, however far above the heads of the majority. Shaw never hesitates to burn his boats by writing plays impossible at the moment: for instance, *Man and Superman* and the Methuselah cycle. He is fond of saying that as playgoers, like other people, hate to be rated as common and lowbrow, they prefer plays that soar above their heads occasionally.

In Shakespeare's time the theatre was really a coterie theatre, frequented and supported by the cultivated aesthetes of the nobility and gentry, and the choice spirits among the groundlings. These latter, of whom there is always a percentage, occupied the bare ground of the roofless pit, while the genteel minority only looked down on their transports, as it were, from the sheltered balconies and even from seats on the stage. So Shakespeare addressed himself to a picked audience. Shaw's audience was much more promiscuous, and the managements much less scholarly. The London theatre-going public of his heyday was not made up of the sort of people most susceptible to his mission.

He educates them in his highbrow prefaces, and gets plenty of fun out of their follies while cultivating them with his plays and living pictures. They have to laugh at themselves. I believe that if either he or Shakespeare stood to-day at the outset of their careers of authorship, *they would write for the screen and never dream of turning back to the limitations of the stage.*[1]

For Bernard Shaw it is, luckily, just not too late to take advantage of the vast opportunities of the new folk-drama medium. From its earliest and crudest beginnings he was intrigued and curious about it, dropping into little back-street, 'flea-pit' cinemas to watch the strange antics of these *parvenu* celluloid celebrities, and find out

[1] NOTE: The words in italics were substituted for my own more hesitant suggestion by Bernard Shaw himself, who edited the opening pages of this chapter.

what, if anything, all the excitement was about. At once he recognised that a revolution in drama and, consequently, in dramatic writing, was on its way. But for a serious, established writer, the time was not yet ripe. Before long, Hollywood was approaching him again and again for the right to film his plays, and offering him fantastic sums for this coveted privilege; but outright, long-distance sales were not what G.B.S. wanted. He wasn't interested in having his plays turned into films by an invisible, uncontrollable process happening thousands of miles away in California. *He* wanted to play with these colossal new toys. He wanted to write for the screen.

It was a great day for the screen when Shaw met Gabriel Pascal. The resulting partnership between them is apt to be regarded as a mere accident, a piece of incredible gipsy-luck for the strange, Continental film-impresario who seemed to have arrived in this country almost by chance, and to have charmed or hypnotised Shaw into yielding the prize on which the hearts of the wealthiest and most powerful Hollywood magnates had been so long set in vain. But Bernard Shaw is not the man to be charmed or hypnotised into doing anything that his reason fails to approve. What he did was not the outcome of a freakish impulse, but a case of instant and unhesitating mutual recognition.

As far as Gabriel Pascal was concerned, the whole thing was a simple case of preordained destiny, so inevitable as almost to be taken for granted, although none the less on that account to be accepted with genuine humility and gratitude. Long ago, in the very early years of this century, as a little, stage-struck, book-devouring boy in Hungary, he had discovered a translated edition of the plays of Bernard Shaw, and enshrined him then and there as the world's greatest dramatic genius, and his own unwitting hero and patron. Later on, when as a young man his enthusiasm for the theatre transferred itself to the more universal, almost wholly unexplored possibilities of picture-making, it became his most cherished ambition to bring Bernard Shaw's plays to the screen; and through years of acting, producing and exhibiting activities in Italy, Germany and France, he nursed the intention, still ardently, in secret.

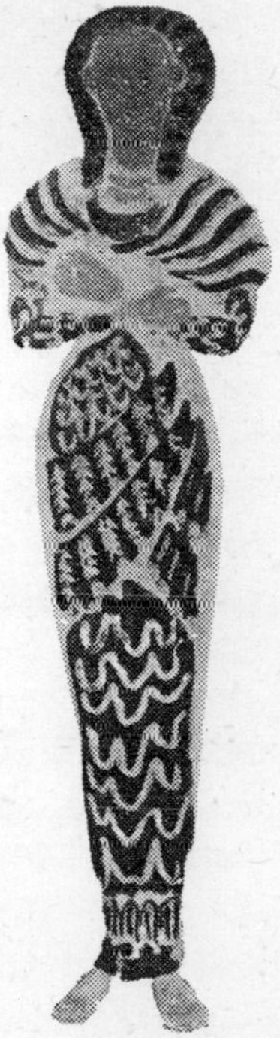

So when, a few days after their historic meeting, Shaw sent Pascal a written agreement to produce film-versions of certain of his plays, it was, for the younger and less famous of the partners, the fulfilment of a lifelong dream. But what was it for Shaw? What did he find in Pascal that inspired him to make this unconsidered, apparently quixotic gesture?

The answer is, again, simple enough, though what is remarkable to me in the whole affair is that G.B.S. should have had the extraordinary penetration or intuition to discover it in the space of one short, and, I should imagine, rather bewildering introductory interview. Pascal is an odd, surprising man to meet for the first time. His English in those days, especially under the pressure of an excited and passionate conviction, must have been more than a little difficult to understand. But Shaw understood him very well.

He must have seen in Pascal a man who believed in every word he, Shaw, had written as profoundly and unshakably as he believed in his own vision of the Shaw plays on the screen; a man of perfect film-sense and artistry, who would yet identify himself wholly with his dramatist's work, and fight with fierce conviction for its true and undiluted reproduction; best of all, a man who understood the plays, not as an intellectual, but with his heart and feelings, and who would somehow find the way to bring out their not always obvious, but never absent, *human* aspect on the screen.

With the production of *Pygmalion*, a new phase of work and creative activity opened up for Bernard Shaw, a phase which continued and intensified through the filming of *Major Barbara* and reached its fullest expression in *Caesar and Cleopatra*. It came at a time when his contacts with the theatre were diminishing. As a stage playwright, Shaw has become an almost legendary figure, and his plays are produced over and over again without making any demands on his constructive or critical powers. Pascal, on the other hand, never stops making demands on them. He neither wishes nor intends to film Shaw's plays without his active collaboration. Every contact with his belovèd G.B.S. is a joy and an inspiration to him, and no detail is too small or unimportant to be made the subject of an appeal to Shavian wisdom. Shaw's replies are prompt, humorous, very much to the point, occasionally sarcastic, but always painstaking. It is obvious that Pascal's queries are matters of equal importance to him.

Extracts from the Shaw-Pascal correspondence during the making of *Caesar and Cleopatra* show plainly the closeness and reality of their collaboration. Shaw's advice is sought in all kinds of matters, including make-up and costume. Britannus, in particular, comes in for a great deal of anxious discussion.

G.B.S. to G.P. 1/7/44.

Britannus is so hopelessly wrong that he will hold up all the scenes in which he appears until he is redressed. I enclose a

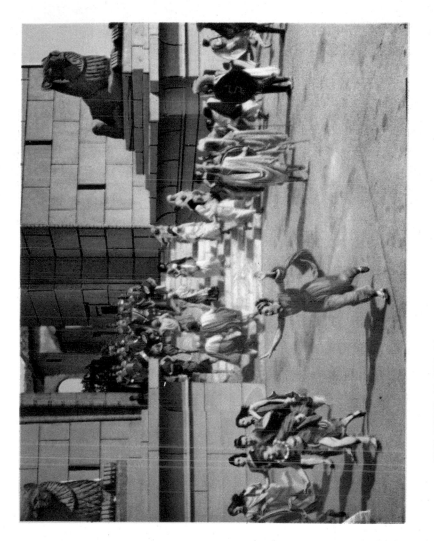

THE ENTRY OF THE ROMAN ARMY CAUSES PANIC AMONGST THE CITIZENS OF ALEXANDRIA

CLEOPATRA BIDS FAREWELL TO CAESAR AND BRITANNUS WHO ARE LEAVING FOR THE BATTLE OF THE PHAROS LIGHTHOUSE

APOLLODORUS, THE YOUNG SICILIAN MERCHANT

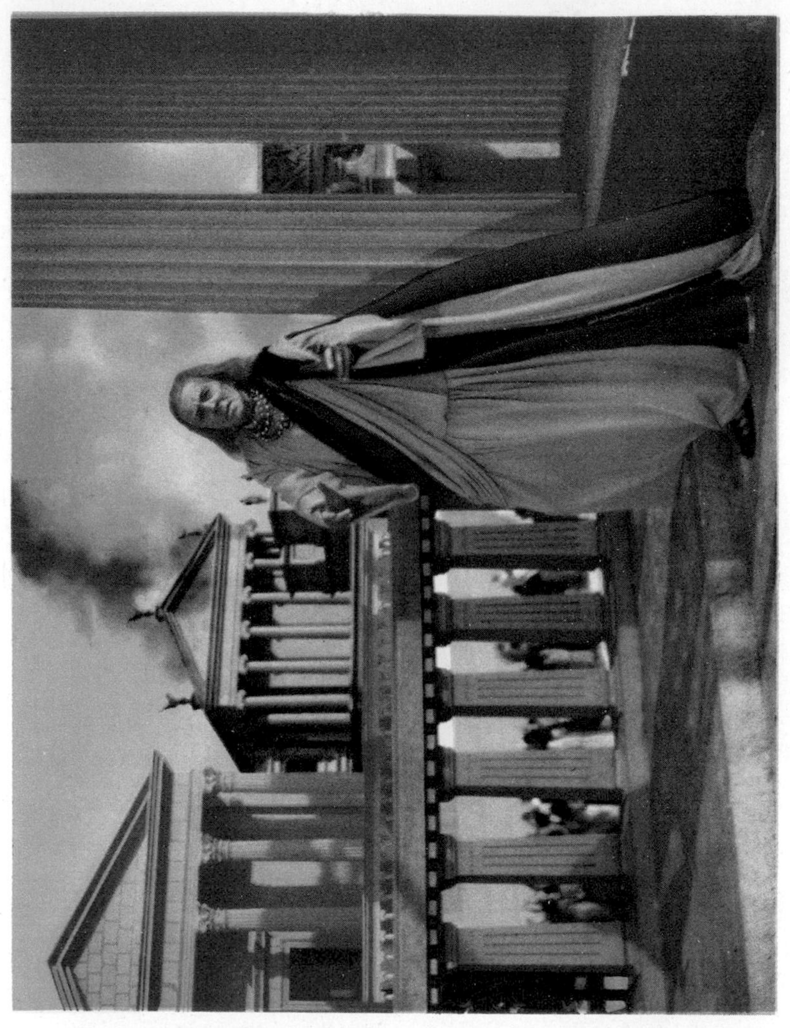

THEODOTUS IS FRANTIC WHEN HE SEES THE BURNING LIBRARY

suggestion of what he should look like. At present he is a handsome young military man instead of an elderly academic literary secretary, very unlike all the others. He must have an academic gown.

G.P. to G.B.S. 8/7/44.
Britannus: since I received your sketch, I have discarded his original costume, which I never liked very much, and have had a long gown made for him; and he will have a kind of shepherd's plaid, which I hope to get next week. I am sending you herewith a photograph of the gown, with a completely different belt, which I hope you will like very much. His wig I have had remade with red hair, as you suggest, and a new moustache, turning down. It is not yet completely to my satisfaction, but they are making a new one which will be nearer to your design.

G.B.S. to G.P. 9/7/44.
Britannus must be mainly in blue: the shepherd's plaid is only for the tunic. That is why the blue overall should be an academic *gown*, opening all down the front. They have plenty of such things in Oxford still.

G.P. to G.B.S. 23/7/44.
I made a new costume, a new wig, and a new moustache for Britannus, and am sending you herewith photos of his costume and make-up. The costume is now a lovely cornflower blue, and the shepherd's plaid hood is checked in pinkish-white and a natural brown, woven in Scotland.

G.B.S. to G.P. 26/7/44.
Dear Gabriel,
Britannus's costume is all right now; but the moustache is hopeless. He must have Dundreary whiskers—yellow whiskers.
In great haste, G.B.S.

(This letter was accompanied by a water-colour sketch of Britannus's head).

G.B.S. to G.P. 28/7/44.
My dear Gabriel,
In the sketch of Britannus I rushed off to you I painted his eyebrows black. They should, of course, be yellow. The wig,

moustache, and whiskers can all be made on a frame which he can put on like a helmet: it cannot be stuck on with spirit gum. The colour should be auburn or downright yellow.

This last, startlingly practical suggestion did not find favour with the Denham make-up department, who were by this time, in any case, somewhat weary of the subject of Britannus's facial accessories. Cecil Parker himself became so depressed by the frequency of Pascal's inspections and infuriated rejections of his make-up, especially of his eyebrows, which were endlessly at fault, that he celebrated their final acceptance in a poem which he called *A Hair-Raising Story*. This tells the tale of all the eyebrows' vicissitudes, from the day on which Pascal first sighted them, when:

> "With mocking tongue and baleful stare,
> He criticised those lumps of hair.
> The right was wrong, the left was right—
> I bore them gently out of sight,
> My eyebrows;"

through the long period of trial and error, when with "blood and toil, tears and sweat, the perfect pair we strove to get;" down to the triumphant occasion on which "the set spun round—for Gaby passed, My eyebrows". The final verse is my favourite:

> "When all things perish, as they must,
> Ash to ash, and dust to dust,
> In heaven I'll blandly meet his gaze,
> I'll smile on him and slowly raise
> My eyebrows."

Even when Britannus, his costume and his make-up, had finally made their united appearance before the camera and thereby been 'established', Pascal's concern about him was not quite at an end, and as late as November the correspondence reverts to him. We were then starting to shoot the Council Chamber scenes, where Britannus makes what is actually his first appearance in the picture, though most of the subsequent sequences had already been shot. It suddenly occurred to Pascal that the impression made by this well-loved character might be improved by the addition of a long shepherd's crook, and G.B.S. was approached by means of a hurried telephone message to Ayot St. Lawrence, requesting his verdict. Back came a beautifully-written postcard, which I reproduce herewith:

From Bernard Shaw.

A crook in England means either a shepherd or a bishop.

Its presence or absence in the film will not affect the receipts by a single centesimo.

Its introduction at so late a stage may involve retakes which will cost J. A. R. thousands of pounds for nothing.

There is no speech in my dialogue so bad that it needs a crook to give it its full value.

A crook is a hindrance to a speaker, and an asset only to a dumb figure in a processional pageant: z.b. a bishop.

Your phoned message leaves me quite in the dark as to who is to wave the crook, or when or where or how or why. It is certainly not worth spending an extra twopence on. G.B.S.

5/11/1944

Undeterred by the mild, but unmistakable signs of exasperation in this response, Pascal supplied Britannus with a crook, and wrote Shaw a reassuring letter:

G.P. to G.B.S. 12/11/44.

My dear G.B.S.,

Don't worry about the crook. Certainly I will not use it through my actor to emphasise any of your lines. I know they don't need any emphasis, and the actor Britannus, Cecil Parker, is the finest understating actor we have, so there is no danger of that at all. Also I won't need any retakes because I only use the crook in the first half of the Council Chamber for his first scenes, and I lose it afterwards.

Costume-details were not, however, the only matters on which Shaw's advice and assistance were sought during production. Details of direction also figure in the correspondence.

G.P. to G.B.S. 8/7/44.

I had a long argument with Claude Rains, who wanted to play the Pharos scene wearing his wreath. My logical argument is that from the moment when Cleopatra puts his helmet on in the Council Chamber, saying " How nice! You look only about fifty in it," he cannot wear anything except the helmet on his head; and the only thing he can do on the Pharos is to take it off and put it down beside him on the faggots, to mop the sweat of African heat from his forehead, so that he can play the carpet scene bareheaded. Then when the tumult is heard in the distance and Caesar turns to Rufio saying: " Come, Rufio," he puts his helmet on again ready for the battle; and only after Apollodorus has made his dive, and he sees there is no other way to escape, he gives his helmet to Britannus, like a gentleman in evening dress handing a *chapeau claque* to his valet, jumps onto the parapet, and dives in himself, bareheaded.

As usual, Shaw replied with verve and alacrity:

G.B.S. to G.P. 9/7/44.

Caesar may be so excited by Apollodorus's dive that he snatches off his helmet and hurls it at Britannus like a ball at cricket; and Britannus fields it like a first-class wicket-keeper.

There is even a Shavian note on diction, headed "The Name Ftatateeta":

Caesar never succeeds in pronouncing this name: he always calls it either Totateeta or Teetatota. But Cleopatra and Ftata herself must speak it clearly and perfectly. To do this they must practise it as Aftatateeta, and when they have got this quite glibly, drop the A.

It will then be as easy as saying " left a message " or " laughed to scorn " or " lift a suitcase " or any other phrase with an ft in it.

The letters refer also to the many difficulties which beset the production, particularly in its opening stages. There was enemy action:

G.P. to G.B.S. 22/6/44.

My dear G.B.S.,

I started shooting on the 12th of this month. During the first week I struggled with great technical difficulties; but I hope to finish the Sphinx sequence next week.

Last Saturday I had a narrow escape on the Pharos set, which is built out of doors on the studio lot, when a flying bomb exploded about 150 yards away in a nearby field. Last night the french windows in my sitting-room on the farm were blown in and the ceiling in my bedroom was cracked completely, so I am having the same gay start on the picture as I had with Major Barbara during the blitz. I hope these pilotless planes are not reaching your district.

I enclose herewith the first batch of stills. I hope you like them.

G.B.S. to G.P. 28/7/44.

Hitler celebrated my birthday by smashing my bedroom window with a bomb; and in the afternoon I had to do a newsreel about it.

And there was action by the oldest of all English enemies—the weather:

G.P. to G.B.S. 23/7/44.

My dearest G.B.S.,

Please forgive me for answering your inspired costume notes only today; but I have had such a hard time fighting against St. Petrus who—coward as he is—has not favoured me with sunshine on the Pharos set. But I am over the worst of it, and at the end of next week I shall start on the Memphis Palace set.

Shaw's visit to the Denham studios during the filming of the Sphinx sequence was followed up by a letter whose general tone, in spite of minor criticisms, was so deeply appreciative and encouraging that Pascal, depressed at this juncture by the initial difficulties of launching such a great production in the post-D-Day atmosphere of national crisis, felt himself inspired afresh.

G.B.S. to G.P. 1/7/44.

My dear Gabriel,

You have surpassed yourself in this production already in one scene. When it is all finished it will lick creation.

There is one thing wrong with the desert sky. The stars and planets are all the same size and brightness, like pinholes. You should have engaged an astronomer to correct this. It is the only thing that gives away the artificiality of the scene.

But I pity poor Rank. The film will cost him a million. On Thursday there were hundreds of men in the studio; and only twelve at most had anything to do but take snapshots and pick up scraps of my conversation for sale to the papers. Most of them did not even do that much. Were they all on the payroll?

However, I am beginning to complain, which is monstrously ungrateful; for the film promises to be a wonder.

Sempre a te,

G.B.S.

Shaw underestimated Pascal only in one respect, that of supposing him capable of overlooking the size or position of a solitary star in his Egyptian firmament! His reply, full of joy and gratitude, hastens to correct this impression.

G.P. to G.B.S. 8/7/44.

My dearest G.B.S.,

Your letter of the 1st July made me very happy, because it gave me hope and assurance that I am on the right road with this production.

Your criticisms are not complaints, but the most creative and helpful suggestions, which I have immediately realised in action.

Regarding the desert sky: you have not seen this in the right light. I not only consulted an astronomical expert, but he designed for us the whole possible sky formation of that period in summertime, which we copied as well as we could. When you see the real sky on the screen, you will be astonished to see how differently it looks from the half-lit sky you saw in the studio, without the reflected clouds which give the sense of distance between the stars. They will not look the same size at all. There are about six different sizes.

Don't worry about poor Rank. Most of the people you saw at the Studio had nothing to do with my unit. They sneaked in from all the other stages to be silent witnesses of the historic moment of your arrival at Denham.

Again, my dearest G.B.S., accept my most affectionate thanks for your visit, and your so helpful suggestions, and your encouraging note, which will be for the whole picture a continuous inspiration, especially in the moments when I am weakened in face of the endless technical difficulties which I must overcome. I realise more than ever during the making of this picture that filming your plays has become my life work, and that you are the greatest inspiration to me in this or any other life.

These selections from a voluminous correspondence give some idea of the scope and nature of Shaw's co-operation on the production itself. His most intensive work of collaboration was, of course, on the preparation of the screen-play and shooting-script, a matter of such peculiar interest to Shaw-lovers that I shall do my best to analyse and illustrate the process in the chapter which follows.

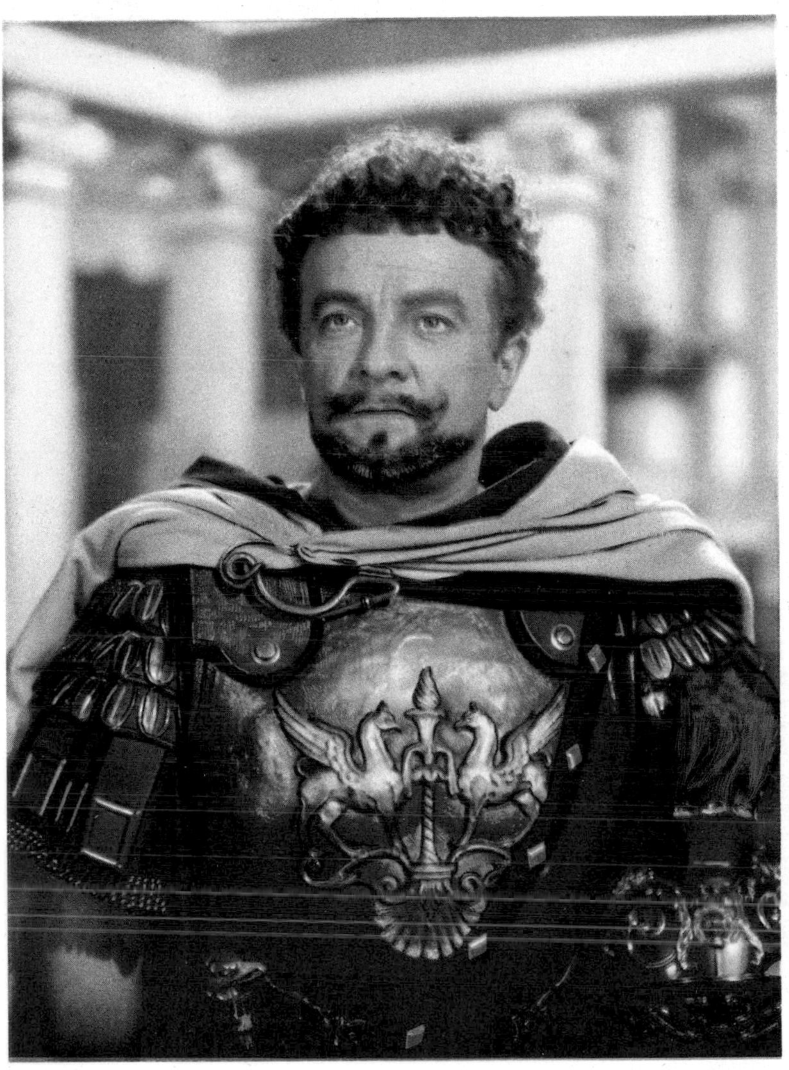

RUFIO, COMRADE-IN-ARMS TO CAESAR

CAESAR TELLS CLEOPATRA THAT THEY MUST LEAVE THE BELEAGUERED PHAROS LIGHTHOUSE

BERNARD SHAW SCREENWRITER

THE curious and striking feature of the play of *Caesar and Cleopatra* is that it might have been written deliberately for the screen.

It reads very much like a film-script. The acts are not formally divided into scenes by the falling of a curtain, but follow one another without any break apart from that provided by a passage of highly imaginative, visual writing, describing the impression to be received by the audience rather than the way in which it is to be obtained. These passages are cinematic in the truest sense of the term.

Take the transition to the Sphinx from the opening scene outside Cleopatra's desert palace, when the courtiers learn that the Queen has disappeared, and that Julius Caesar and his Roman legions are rapidly approaching. Shaw ends the scene with these words:

"General panic. They all fly with cries of consternation. The torch is thrown down and extinguished in the rush. Darkness. The noise of the fugitives dies away. Dead silence. Suspense. Then the blackness and stillness break softly into silver mist and strange airs as the wind-swept harp of Memnon plays at the dawning of the moon. It rises full over the desert; and a vast horizon comes into relief, broken by a huge shape which soon reveals itself in the spreading radiance as a Sphinx pedestalled on the sands."

What is this but a singularly poetic description of a fade-out, both of sound and picture, from one scene, and of a fade-in to the next?

Again, the change of scene from the Sphinx back to the Palace is described in terms much more obviously fitted to the technique of the screen than of the stage:

"He follows her, the bucina sounding louder as they steal across the desert. The moonlight wanes: the horizon again shows black against the sky, broken only by the fantastic silhouette of the Sphinx. The sky itself vanishes in darkness, from which there is no relief until the gleam of a distant torch falls on great Egyptian pillars supporting the roof of a majestic corridor. At the further end of this corridor a Nubian slave appears, carrying the torch. Caesar, still led by Cleopatra, follows him."

My fellow screen-writers, please read, mark and learn! Notwithstanding the fact that all this was written for the stage round about the year 1900, this is *how* to write for the screen! When we can express ourselves one-half as beautifully as this, yet with the same perfectly simple clarity of vision, we shall be worthy followers of our profession. Even though our work is seldom, if ever, published, though the multigraphed records of our labours, tattered and dog-eared from countless hurried thumbings of script-girls, assistant-directors and technicians in search of executive guidance, pile up dustily on forgotten shelves at Elstree and Denham, we must not be content to clothe our ideas in drab, perfunctory, carelessly chosen words. They must supply the quickening flame which is to kindle the imagination of all the creative workers on the production—the director, the actors, the musical composer, the designers. How can they do that if they themselves are not aglow?

Hear how Shaw instructs the art-director concerning this same entrance to Cleopatra's palace:

"They come down the corridor, Caesar peering keenly about at the strange architecture, and at the pillars' shadows between which, as the passing torch makes them hurry noiselessly backwards, figures of men with wings and hawks' heads, and vast black marble cats, seem to flit in and out of ambush."

Who has not been a timid child, going to bed by candlelight through strange passages and stairways, nor can fail to be stirred by the lovely imagery of that description? But expressed in the banal language of an ordinary film-scenario, what is left of the true spirit of picture-making?

INT. CORRIDOR OF PALACE. NIGHT.

This is a pillared corridor, decorated with ancient Egyptian statues of an early period.

L.S. CAESAR, CLEOPATRA AND NUBIAN SLAVE.

Caesar, Cleopatra and slave enter R. of camera, and come down the corridor. The slave goes ahead, carrying a torch. Caesar and Cleopatra follow him.

It is all perfectly correct and businesslike, but it is not *alive*. It is the tremendous vitality of Shaw's pictorial language, quite apart from the brilliance of his dialogue, which makes him, for me, such an inspired and inspiring scenarist.

The fact that the play of *Caesar and Cleopatra* is so richly endowed with this intrinsic cinematic quality meant that its screen-adaptation did not call for the addition of nearly so much new material as had been the case with its predecessor, *Major Barbara*, for which Shaw wrote no less than ten new dialogue scenes. He wrote only two additional scenes for *Pygmalion*, the famous glimpse of Eliza in the bath-tub, and some lines for the big reception sequence; but Pascal had to play the latter almost as a ballet-episode, with music and practically without audible spoken comment, in order to get round the fact that he had not sufficient appropriate Shavian dialogue. This may have been another instance

of Shaw's unerring musical instinct, because the result was to enhance the dreamlike atmosphere of Cinderella-at-the-Ball.

For *Caesar and Cleopatra* only one new scene was agreed upon by Shaw and Pascal to begin with. This is the scene in Cleopatra's bedroom in the Palace at Alexandria, where she wakes up on the morning after her arrival, realising afresh all the splendid and delightful possibilities of her queenly situation, and asks her nurse, Ftatateeta: "What will Caesar do with me, now I am a Queen?"

"Ask rather what you will do with him," says Ftatateeta, relishing in every female, feline fibre the new prospects of palace intrigue and indirect power-politics which she sees opening up before herself and her young charge. "My child, you have charmed him. You are safe: you are powerful. I will guide you until you learn how to guide yourself."

This scene, inserted primarily to establish a time-lapse of twenty-four hours while both sides prepare their strategy, Caesar and his followers inside the Palace, and the Egyptians outside it, provides also a welcome change of background and mood after the strongly dramatic "occupation" episode in the Council Chamber. It gives an opportunity also, to the composer, Georges Auric, to introduce a new lullaby theme, and for this, too, Shaw supplies verbal inspiration. Here are the words in which he introduces the new scene:

"The moon, accompanied by the nocturne music, passes across the screen to the west to indicate the passing of the night. The music is broken twice by a syncopated throb and flash of summer lightning. Towards the end of the transit the moon fades; the sky brightens into dawning sunlight; and the oboe cuts in with a pastoral descant. Tall, straight lines of buildings appear, with appropriate chords from the wind; and the scene dissolves into Cleopatra's bedchamber and the music into a lullaby. Cleopatra is seen fast asleep in bed for long enough to let the audience take in the whole change.

"The lullaby is interrupted by a brilliant reveillé from the Roman military trumpets under the windows outside. This finishes the music. Cleopatra, rudely awakened, sits up with her knees under her chin, rubbing her eyes."

CLEOPATRA:

(*calling*)

Ftatateeta! Ftatateeta!

This grasp of the screen-dramatist's task as a composition in terms of music and vision combined shows itself over and over again in Shaw's work on the *Caesar and Cleopatra* scenario. Unmistakably, the imaginative film-performance which plays itself inside his brain as he thinks of what he will write, is not seen merely in patterns of light and shade and speech and movement, but of fully-orchestrated music as well! "Tall straight lines of buildings appear, with appropriate chords from the wind . . ." The buildings, occurring almost casually like that in the midst of a dissolve, seem to be there to express the very *shape of the sound.*

I find this exciting. It is new. It makes me want to write and make films in a quite new way. Is it not clear that this 89-year-old man, turning his mind half-reluctantly to an unfamiliar task, has outstripped all the most highly-trained and experienced screen-writers at one bound, and indicated the writing of film-drama on an altogether new aural and visual level?

There was another point in the scenario at which Pascal—and I, too—badly wanted a new scene, but G.B.S. was unwilling to give it to us. This was to bridge the six months' interval between Acts III and IV, and is explained in a letter from Pascal to Shaw, written during the making of the picture:

G.P. to G.B.S. 23/7/44.

Incidentally, when I come to the Music Room sequence, reading from the play and the script, I always have the feeling that a very short new scene would be useful to bridge the time gap of six months since the foregoing scene on the Pharos. You start Act IV with the following statement: "Cleopatra's sousing in the east harbour of Alexandria was in October 48 B.C. In March 47 she is passing the afternoon in her boudoir in the palace." It is this interval that I want to cover smoothly on the screen, instead of leaving the audience in ignorance of the time-situation until Cleopatra tells Pothinus: "These six months we have been besieged in the palace by my subjects."

To this Shaw replies non-committally:

G.B.S. to G.P. 28/7/44.

I think there must be a definite break in the continuity after the lighthouse scene; but I will study it and see what can be done with the help of your suggestions.

Reflection on both sides merely strengthened their respective viewpoints. Pascal was sure there should be a new scene, establishing in a few lines of dialogue what had happened in the six months' interval, but he could not rouse Shaw's enthusiasm. We sent him several suggestions, none of which met with his approval; and when, a whole year later, he was finally persuaded to write a most delightful comedy scene in a barber's shop with Rufio coming to have his hair and beard attended to before Cleopatra's banquet, a regular conspiracy of misfortune prevented its production. Since we no longer had any studio-space, the Barber's Shop set was built out-of-doors, in one corner of the huge Denham lot where the crowd and action scenes were made during the summer of 1945, a year after the production of the main part of the picture;

CLEOPATRA ON THE PAW OF HER FAVOURITE SPHINX

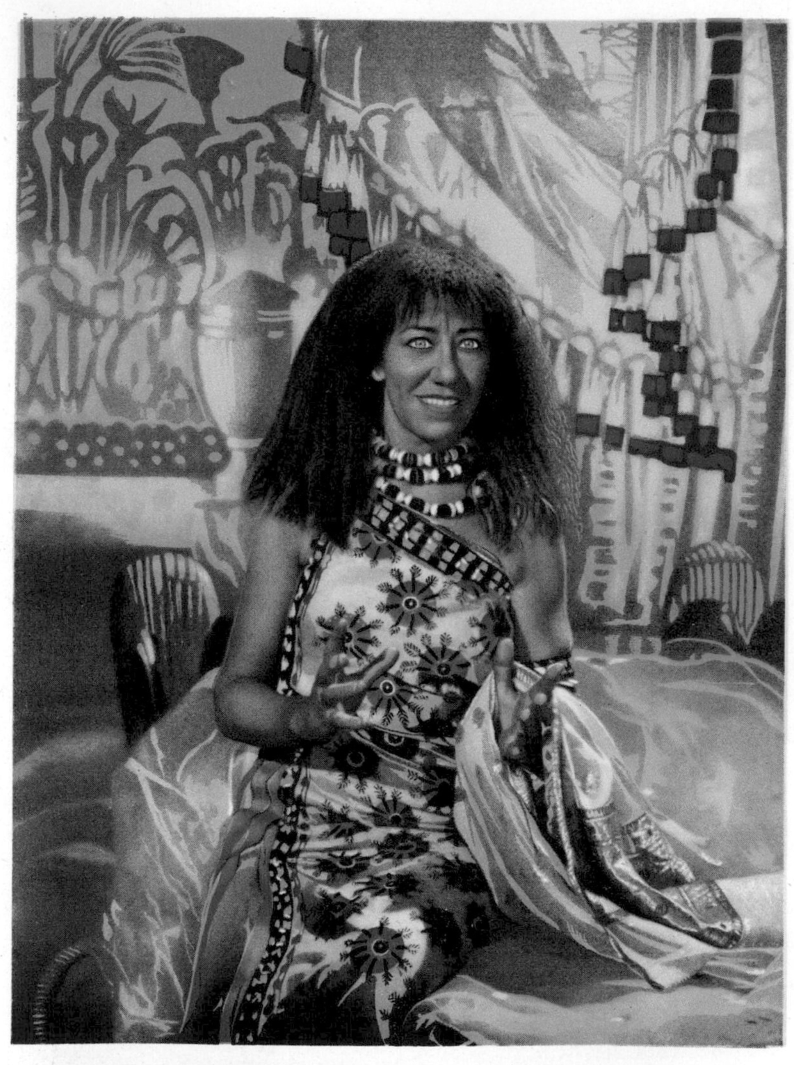

FTATATEETA, NURSE TO CLEOPATRA, IN THE QUEEN'S BEDROOM

and the "cowardice of St. Petrus", or, more prosaically, the almost total lack of sunshine during this production-aftermath, held up Pascal's work to such an extent that, by the time we got to the Barber's Shop scene, its key character, Basil Sydney, was no longer available.

The scene as it stood had therefore to be abandoned, and we fell back on Shaw's alternative suggestion for leading into Act V, which shows the old musician and the harpist-girl approaching the Palace, "she on a handsome Bactrian camel, half caged in red curtains: he on a well-caparisoned ass." The lovely little Barber's Shop set was, however, to use Pascal's own words, "cheated in" in the background, and a phrase or two of the original scene salvaged, so that all was not quite lost. Moreover, the entire scene, exactly as Shaw wrote it, is reproduced by his kind permission on pp. 62–64 of this book.

A red ink note, written in Shaw's own handwriting at the top of his typescript of the Barber's Shop scene, supplies another excellent example of his inherent sense of film technique. It had been tentatively suggested that the end of the Pharos sequence, showing Caesar, with Cleopatra on his back, swimming for the galleys, should connect with the new scene by means of a trick dissolve, the water of Alexandria harbour changing into water in a bowl in the Barber's Shop. Such a dissolve at this point would be not only old-fashioned and distracting, but fundamentally incorrect. The swimming episode closes a long, complete, narrative sequence, and must, therefore, end in a fade-out, with the following sequence fading in on something quite fresh, unrelated to the previous scene either by picture or sound. G.B.S.'s vigorous red ink note shows his immediate and scornful repudiation of the suggested error:

"There must be no camera tricks in the changes, nothing *unnatural*. The fading out of the lighthouse and the sea may be slow and accompanied by music or distant shouting, but the Barber's Shop must appear instantaneously, fully lighted, with a clash of the full orchestra, cymbals fortissimo, quite frankly, without any attempt to make the change gradual. The atmosphere must be cleared with a bang for a fresh start. The suggested tricks with a basin and sponge appearing first are quite damnable: they would give away the illusion of reality and change the play into an exhibition of camera conjuring."

Here again he is thinking musically. It seems that every time he puts his mind to a problem of film composition, it presents itself to him in terms of music and light combined.

The only other new scene written by Shaw for the film version of *Caesar and Cleopatra* is the one showing the first entry of the Roman troops into Alexandria. Pascal had intended to show the occupation without actual dialogue, but in talking it over with G.B.S. he asked him for some lines for Egyptian bystanders, and for the Roman officer in charge of the troops. Instead of a few lines we received a complete scene, which, brief as it is, has become to my mind one of the most vital and cinematic of the whole picture. Its opening passage provides another illustration of Shaw's unique quality as a screen-writer:

"Noise outside: first the Roman trumpets: then the Alexandrian mob flying in terror, expressed by hurried music, culminating in the appearance on the screen of the street with the people running away in all directions, hiding where they can or crowding against the houses to leave the road clear for a column of Roman soldiers marching with a discipline which contrasts strongly with the disorder of the crowd. The Centurion, cudgel in hand, marches beside the files. The buglers and drummers are at the head of the column. Quick march. Meanwhile, the crowd as it flies shouts inarticulately while it is in motion."

So much—and it is plenty—to quicken the imagination of the director. As soon as he had the occupying troops

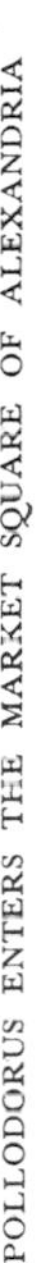

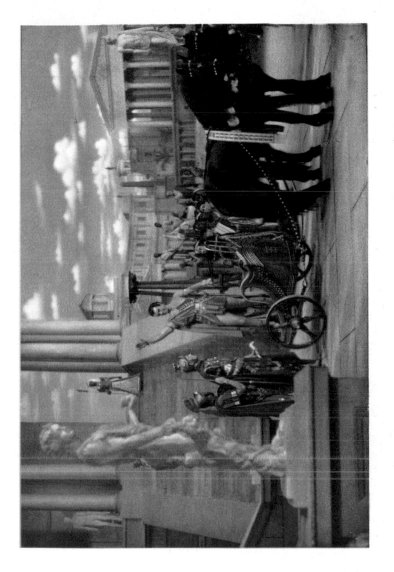

APOLLODORUS ENTERS THE MARKET SQUARE OF ALEXANDRIA

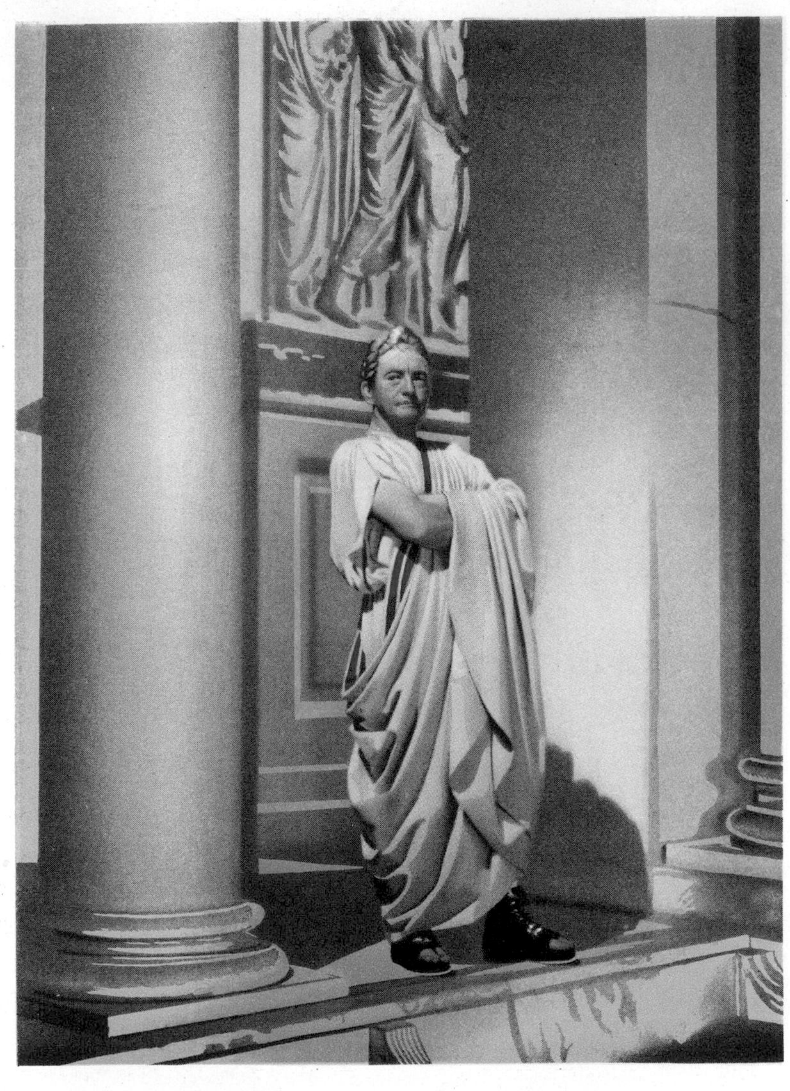

CAESAR IN THE COUNCIL CHAMBER OF THE PALACE OF ALEXANDRIA

THE BOY KING PTOLEMY AND HIS GUARDIAN POTHINUS

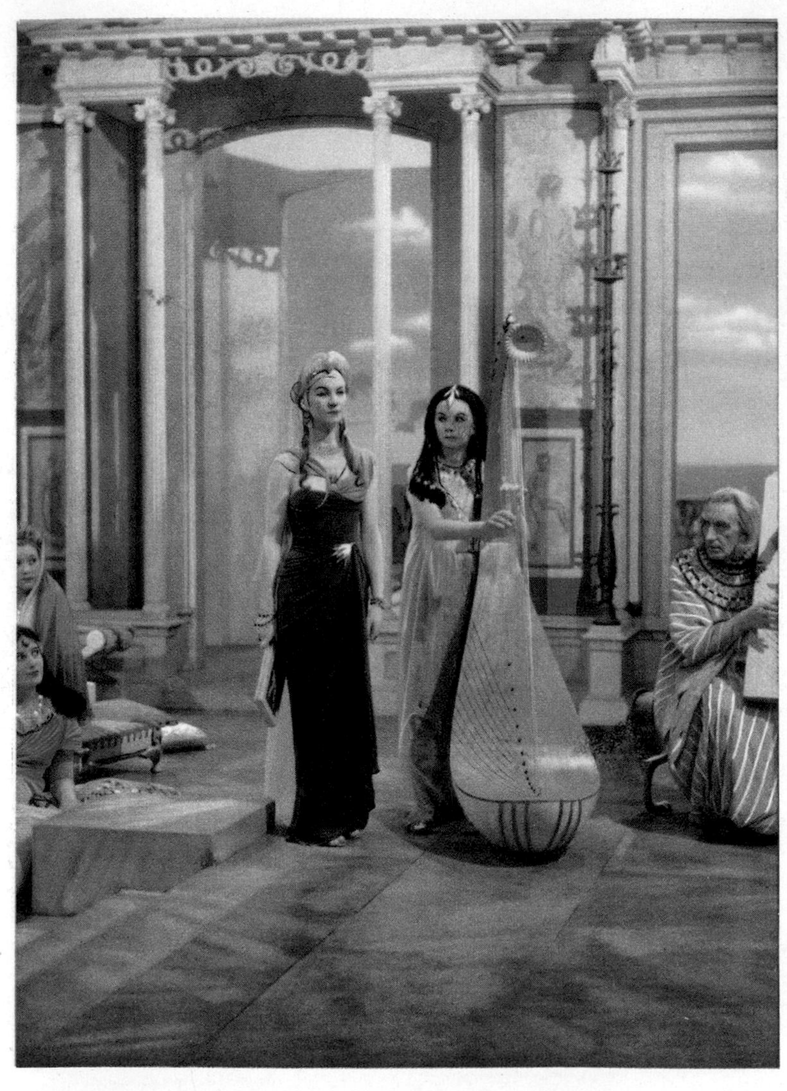

CLEOPATRA IN HER MUSIC ROOM, WITH THE YOUNG GIRL HARPIST

drawn up in formation on the main square, Shaw provides the officer in charge, played by Michael Rennie, with a most topical witticism in the course of his instructions to the men:

OFFICER (*to the troops*): This city is Alexandria. Remember that: Al-ex-andria, the Egyptian capital. You've got to behave yourselves here. Be stiffish with the men: but you may fraternize with the women. (*A big laugh from the troops.*) Silence! Silence, I tell you.

What a joy for a producer to have his scenario suggestions rewarded by scenes and lines like these! It looks so easy, this gift of straightforward, graphic film expression. In fact, it is so rare. I confess to the heresy of wishing that G.B.S. had devoted only half his literary lifetime to his plays, and had spent all the rest of it in writing for the screen.

THE BARBER'S SHOP
THE UNSHOT SCENE

A BARBER's shop in Alexandria. The barber is operating on a customer wrapped in the usual surplice. He has almost finished with him, and is holding two bronze mirrors (looking-glasses having not yet been invented) so that the customer can see the back of his head.

BARBER: How is that, Excellency?

CUSTOMER: Perfect.

BARBER (*putting aside the mirrors*): Brilliantine?

CUSTOMER: Yes: plenty of it. But not the perfumed sort.

BARBER (*applying the wash and brushing it in*): I understand, Excellency. A royal major domo must be neutral. If you have the same scent as a courtier he thinks you have stolen it from him.

CUSTOMER: True. I meet nobody but courtiers: you meet all sorts. These Romans now. What do you make of them?

BARBER: To a barber, Excellency, all men are alike. Romans, Greeks, Egyptians, Jews wear the same robe in my chair and say the same things. Fair or dark, the same scissors cuts them all. What can you say of any man but that he is a man?

CUSTOMER: But these Romans are barbarians: they burn our library, one of the seven wonders of the world. They are magicians: they dig wells in the salt sand and draw fresh water from them. Their biggest and heaviest men swim like dolphins and carry the Queen on their backs.

BARBER: That might be the Queen's magic. She rides on Caesar's back now, on land as on the sea. She has made him king here these six months.

CUSTOMER: Do not believe it. He has made her Queen.

BARBER: One good turn deserves another. But I know nothing about women: I am not a lady's hairdresser.

CUSTOMER: And all Romans are alike to you?

BARBER: All men are alike to me.

CUSTOMER: You would not say that if you knew Caesar and his henchman Rufio.

BARBER: Ah, I forgot Rufio. You are right, Excellency: no other man alive has such whiskers. My one professional ambition is to shave them off and make him look like a human being.

Rufio strides in.

RUFIO: You are engaged. How soon will you be free?

BARBER: Your worship's name was the last word in our mouths. Three minutes, general: not a moment more.

CUSTOMER: Don't you recognise me in this gown?

RUFIO: What! The royal major domo! I crave your pardon: I have seen you only in your court splendour.

CUSTOMER (*to the barber*): Finish up quickly. Do not keep the general waiting.

RUFIO: Take it easy: I am in no hurry.

CUSTOMER: You are a busy man, general: always in a hurry. (*To the Barber, rising*) *:* There: that's enough. *He throws off his gown and stands in his breeches and singlet until the Barber fetches his official coat and arrays him in his courtly magnificence. Rufio throws himself into the vacated chair.*

RUFIO: Now you look like yourself, major. (*The Barber approaches him with the surplice*) *:* No gown for me. Take it away.

BARBER: But, general, the cut whiskers will be all over your clothes.

RUFIO: Cut a single hair of my whiskers and I will cut your thumbs off. Let my whiskers alone. Attend to my hair.

BARBER (*disappointed*, *pitifully*): Oh, general, I had set my heart on your whiskers.

RUFIO: You would. Your Queen says they remind her of a lousy bird's nest. I have to banquet with her and with Caesar this afternoon. Make them look glossy and smell nice.

CUSTOMER: I must take my leave, general. I also have to be on duty at the banquet. Au revoir.

RUFIO (*offhandedly*): Good afternoon.

The customer goes out, giving a coin to the Barber as he passes.

BARBER (*half voice*): A thousand thanks, Excellency. (*He bows the customer out and returns to the chair.*) Nobody in Alexandria under sixty lets hair grow on his face, general. Can I not persuade you to have them off?

RUFIO: Have them off! What should I look like without them? My authority is in them. I should look like that bumptious noodle who has just left us. Do as I tell you and look sharp about it.

The Barber, with a sigh, resigns himself to his task.

The scene fades out. Act IV of the printed play follows.

VIVIEN LEIGH'S CLEOPATRA

When Bernard Shaw heard that Vivien Leigh had always hankered after the part of Cleopatra in his play, he asked how old she was, and looked surprised at the answer.

"And is she very tall and stout?"

When told that she was neither, but, on the contrary, remarkably small and slender, he seemed more astonished than ever.

"I ask because it is a curious fact that the ladies who set their hearts on that particular rôle are invariably giantesses of over fifty. Miss Leigh must be exceptional."

Miss Leigh is, and always has been, exceptional, the darling of destiny and circumstance alike. Not only beautiful but graceful as well, and highly intelligent into the bargain, one cannot imagine that she should ever have had to struggle and agonise to make her way in life. Success must have come to her easily, naturally; certainly not without plenty of hard work, but without the endless set-backs and disappointments which are the lot of so many members of the acting profession. The result is a personality which is notably clear and unshadowed, giving a brilliant, princesslike quality of assurance and poise which, for the part of Cleopatra, has an obvious value.

Every inspired actor or actress has one ideal rôle on which his heart is set, one cherished portrayal which seems to him exclusively and rightfully his own. Shaw's Cleopatra was that rôle for Vivien Leigh. She knew she could *be* that lovely, naïve, catlike creature—inquisitive and greedy and cruel, yet with such a noble capacity for passion and proudly loyal love that she ends by catching at one's heart. Among Gabriel Pascal's foremost reasons for embarking on such a great picture as *Caesar and Cleopatra* at such a difficult time was the fact that Vivien Leigh was here in England, free and willing to star in it.

After *Gone With the Wind* and *Lady Hamilton*, she had disappeared for three years from the screen. Living in England to be near her husband, Laurence Olivier, during his term of national service, she was, inevitably, pursued by screen offers; but she refused them all. There was only one film part she really wanted: Cleopatra in Shaw's play.

To watch her work on the picture was, to me, a fascinating experience. Everything she did seemed effortless, but perfectly timed and final. One is used, during rehearsals, to seeing actors grope after the proper co-ordination of words and movements, trying them over and over again before they can achieve the right effect. Vivien Leigh never seemed to pass through these experimental stages. Laying aside a blue satin dressing-gown and a crossword puzzle, she would take her place before the camera, and be, instantly, not Vivien Leigh at all, but Cleopatra, matching gestures and dialogue with grace and accuracy, and repeating them, when called upon, again and again and again with the same tireless certainty and rhythm.

Take the scene iu the Memphis Palace, where she pulls herself away from Caesar, beats the slave, chases him, throws away the whip, and then skims the whole length of the throne room to leap on to the dais, wave her arms above her head and cry exultantly: "I am a Queen at last—a real, real Queen! Cleopatra the Queen!" The most experienced players would expect to have to rehearse such a complicated scene many times before they could be sure of being in the right place at the right moment, and of finishing exactly in front of the throne. Vivien Leigh did it all unerringly the first time she tried the scene, and subsequent rehearsals were more for the benefit of the camera and the technical staff generally than from any need to improve on her performance.

The question was whether on top of all this efficiency and aptitude for presenting the childish, half-savage side of Cleopatra's character, she was capable also of suggesting the latent, developing qualities of maturity and passion called for by the latter part of the play. Her greatest screen-parts hitherto have not made very exacting psychological demands. The most striking thing, perhaps, about Scarlett O'Hara is that experience does not change her; and though Lady Hamilton suffers and matures, the character-development is of a rather passive kind. The exciting thing about Shaw's Cleopatra is that you watch the process by which a child turns into a woman, and a foolish nursery-kitten into a highly controlled and dominating queen. Could Vivien Leigh interpret that transforming experience? Could she show us the struggle and emotional strife through which alone it could take place?

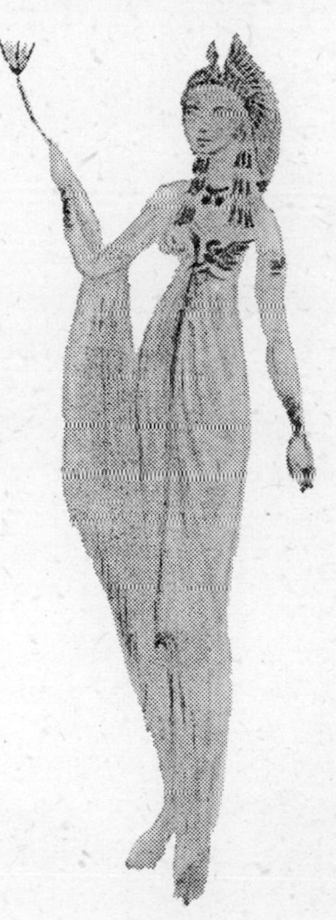

I think she has done so triumphantly. The scenes at the banquet on the roof of the Palace, where Pothinus accuses her of treachery to Caesar and she orders his death in revenge, are to my mind the most finely-acted in the picture, and Vivien Leigh's performance in these scenes, suddenly taking on a quite new range and depth, is a moving thing to see. It is a joy to watch her first of all trying to conceal from Caesar what she has done, falling back on old childish tricks of coquetry and artifice, shedding them a moment later to protest her personal loyalty, and then, hardened and humiliated by his disbelief, all at once confessing her action with regal pride: "He was slain by order of the Queen of Egypt!"

And in the final scene of the picture, when she waves farewell to Caesar, smiling and crying all in the same moment, I believe the audience will find themselves in exactly the same confusion, divided between laughter and tears.

What a part for a great actress! But then, too, what a great actress for the part!

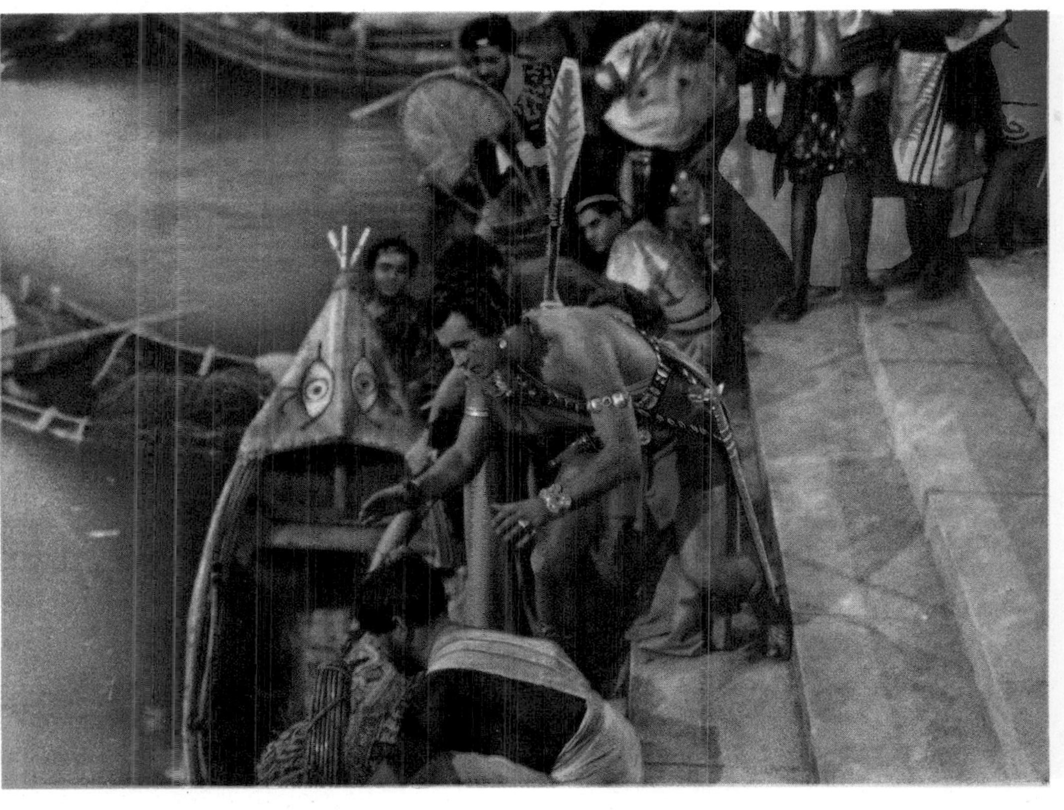

APOLLODORUS TAKES A PRESENT IN THE FORM OF A BUNDLE OF CARPETS TO CAESAR ON THE PHAROS LIGHTHOUSE

CLAUDE RAINS' CAESAR

Claude Rains was in the nature of a *sine qua non* for the film of *Caesar and Cleopatra*, because it is so hard to imagine who could have played Caesar if he had not done so.

"But who is to play Caesar?" sighed Vivien Leigh, lamenting the fact that she wanted to play Cleopatra soon, *soon*—but where was a Caesar to be found?

And: "But there is no Caesar, is there?" said Mrs. Shaw, hearing the subject discussed between Pascal and her husband; and her question was put in the very positive way referred to in Latin grammar-books as "expecting the answer 'No'."

The part was originally played—"created" is the somewhat lavish term used by the acting profession to describe such a classic first performance—by Forbes Robertson. To have seen Forbes Robertson's Caesar is a high claim to audience-distinction. Sam Behrmann, America's brilliant comedy-dramatist, told me that, as a small boy, he managed to save up enough money to buy a ticket for the first night of a one-week provincial performance of the play during the famous actor's American tour, and was so passionately impressed that he somehow contrived to see it again each night for the rest of the week.

Any more recent rendering of Caesar has thus been to some extent haunted and overshadowed by memories of Forbes Robertson's wonderful voice and classic profile, giving the rôle a noble dignity of bearing which is, to my mind, not really demanded by—nor even entirely suited to—the character of Caesar as Shaw has portrayed him. It needed to be played, not better, but altogether differently, to be realised afresh. And the moment Pascal announced

Claude Rains as his ideal choice for the part, it was apparent that here would be quite a new Caesar, evoking no reminiscent echoes, but informing the part with an inner life and vigour of its own.

Not merely in his dramatic style, but in his personal history, Claude Rains supplies a link between two schools of acting: the old Irving-Tree-Forbes-Robertson school of grand drama, expressing itself in a freedom of voice and gesture which would nowadays strike us as unreal; and the modern stylised school of dramatic under-statement, of which Gerald du Maurier was the first really successful exponent in this country, to be followed and perfected by such nonchalant, polished actors as Leslie Howard and Felix Aylmer. (Incidentally, Gabriel Pascal has a theory that the contemporary theatre, led by Ralph Richardson and Laurence Olivier, is now swinging back in the opposite direction, towards a more robust form of dramatic expression.)

Rains was in fact trained as an actor by Beerbohm Tree, whose company he joined, first as a call-boy, then as stage-manager, finally as an actor himself, in the great Tree-Terry days at the Haymarket. Bernard Shaw remembers him there, and afterwards, as a fine, intelligent actor, too little noticed by the English theatre critics and public, before his disappearance from our stage and subsequent re-emergence as a front-rank film actor in Hollywood.

There, in brief, is Claude Rains' acting background. Professionally, he is not an easy man to deal with. One has the impression, indeed, that he has never found himself easy to deal with! He has none of Vivien Leigh's facility and grace. Rains has always worked hard at his acting, and now that he is an established star he continues to work hard at it. But out of his personal and histrionic struggles there emerges a genuine power. His Caesar has recognisable greatness. Here is the small, ageing, heroic man, happiest in action and the brotherhood of military comradeship, yet most truly himself in solitude, in the half-melancholy philosophy of a declining age, and the scornful clemency for which he was as much hated as renowned.

The whole performance builds up an unforgettable personality. Whether he is gay and carefree, wasting time over Cleopatra's childish pranks—"fooling with this girl here!" cries the exasperated Rufio—on the Pharos, or reluctantly romantic at the Sphinx, or "idle, luxurious and kind" at Cleopatra's banquet, or sternly unforgiving as he confronts its murderous sequel, he is always the same vital, utterly characteristic Caesar, a man we know and can understand even when his actions momentarily defeat us. And underlying everything he says and does is a fundamental quality of humorous resourcefulness, expressing itself in the lifting of an eyebrow, a quickly-suppressed grin, a sudden mock solemnity. This is Shavian acting of a high order.

I wish I had seen Forbes Robertson's Caesar for its sheer beauty, the music of its speech to the Sphinx, and all the elegance and eloquence of a lost acting tradition. But I rejoice to have seen Claude Rains' Caesar for its dry subtlety and strength, the curious sense it gives one of a great man's essential loneliness and isolation.

When Pascal took Rains to Ayot St. Lawrence a few days after his arrival in this country, he made an instantaneously favourable impression. In a letter to Pascal a few days afterwards, Shaw said: "I remembered him and was perfectly satisfied in the first split second."

And I believe this Shavian testimonial will be echoed by thousands of Claude Rains' admirers all over the world, meeting him as Caesar at the Sphinx.

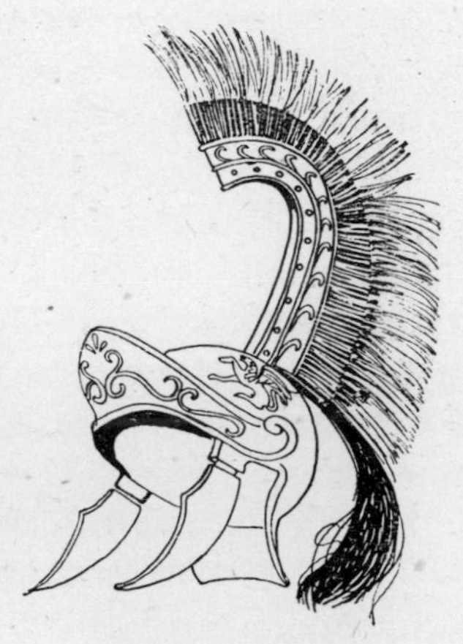

THE PLAYERS

A LARGE cast always sets the producer of a picture an appalling jigsaw-puzzle problem when the time comes to decide on the exact alignment of the artists' credits. To avoid involving myself in anything of the sort, I have arranged Shaw's principal characters in alphabetical order, without any reference to their dramatic or professional importance, and I hope I may be forgiven for thus dealing with them in turn.

"A" first, then, for Achillas and Apollodorus.

Achillas is played by a newcomer to the screen, Antony Eustrel. Pascal saw him in a series of Shakespearean rôles at the Stratford-on-Avon Festival, and congratulated himself on having discovered a coming actor with the poise and maturity that is called for by this brief, but very difficult and dramatically important part. Achillas is Caesar's military antagonist. They come face to face in the Council Chamber, and cross swords in a swift and bitter dialogue exchange. The younger man's attitude is arrogant and assured. Caesar's smiling, mildly sarcastic courtesy seeks to outface him; but at this point it must fail to do so. Achillas remains defiant and unsubdued, conveying to the audience a dramatic threat of what Caesar is up against in his risky, impudent strategy, and continuing thus in their minds, though he never reappears in the play, through the scenes that follow.

A well-known and highly accomplished actor, approached earlier by Pascal to play Achillas, refused the part because, he said, he knew he could not hope to stand up to Claude Rains in the verbal duel of that Council Chamber scene. But Antony Eustrel did not hesitate, and there was no need for him to do so. His scene with Rains achieves, for the character of Achillas and the unfolding of the drama, all that Shaw meant it to do.

Apollodorus is described by Shaw as "a dashing young man of about twenty-four, handsome and debonair, dressed with deliberate aestheticism". The part is apt to be allotted to the more effeminate type of juvenile, but Gabriel Pascal does not like effeminate juveniles, and he wanted Apollodorus to be played by the most virile, athletic, young male actor in this country. It did not take him long to decide that Stewart Granger was the answer to his requirements, though the more conventionally-minded among his associates were inclined to question the choice.

The part is not an easy one to play. It is never suggested that Cleopatra wastes a tender or romantic thought on her admirer, while she makes use of him shamelessly to pursue her ends with Caesar. But Granger's Apollodorus imbues the rôle with so much physical splendour and *joie de vivre* that one accepts his devotion to Cleopatra as a kind of light-hearted gallantry which never even threatens to become oppressive. Watching him cross swords with the Roman sentries, soar above the Pharos swinging airily from the crane, or dive like a swallow into the harbour far below, dressed always in the gay, brilliant clothes Messel designed for him as being more suited to his flamboyant physique than the pale half-tones envisaged for this character by Shaw, the audience can momentarily resign their mental appreciation of the drama to a purely visual joy in the beauty of colour and movement. He has the gaiety, the insensitive heartlessness of a superb young animal. I am not at all sure that he is what Shaw meant by the character; but he is what Pascal means, and I find it an unqualified success.

Pascal's casting of *Britannus* came again as something of a surprise to Shavian conventionalists. This rôle

supplies the comedy relief in Shaw's drama, and it was expected that it would be played by a well-known comedian. Cecil Parker has never been regarded as a comedian, but as a "straight" character-actor of a rather serious and sensitive type. His Britannus capitalises this natural gravity in an extraordinary way. It gives the whole character the true essence of comedy, mingling a curious vein of pity with the laughter it evokes in the onlooker. There is such an endearing quality in the man's pomposity, and withal so much true dignity and pride in his devotion to his "great master", that we share Caesar's delight in his British slave, and endorse his final decision not to part with him "for a million talents". All these sentiments are, of course, inherent in the part as Shaw wrote it, but Cecil Parker's performance, giving the very priggishness of Britannus a certain grace, a *charm* that seems inseparable from the noble solemnity of his features, seems to catch the dramatist's meaning so exactly that I find myself unable to imagine any other actor in his place:

The *Ftatateeta* of Flora Robson, on the other hand, tends to diminish rather than to heighten the comedy-angle of the part as Shaw originally conceived it. Hers is a primitive, barbaric interpretation, producing excitement rather than amusement in the audience. Her moments of humiliation at Caesar's hands, and the terror she strikes into the hearts of the Roman sentries, are thus not so intrinsically funny as they might have been, given a broader, more farcical rendering of the rôle. But this loss of comedy is, I think, a gain in dramatic value, imparting to the latter scenes of the film, and the whole build-up to the assassination of Pothinus, a fierce,

fearsome quality, which might have been weakened by stronger hilarity associations with the person of Ftatateeta.

Her appearance in itself is superb, the dark make-up and heavy mop of black hair, allied with the rich sombre colourings of her tightly-swathed garments, giving her the lithe, savage impression of a tigress. Once again, this does not quite tally with Shaw's original vision of the character in his play, which introduces Ftatateeta as "a huge, grim woman, her face covered with a network of tiny wrinkles, and her eyes old, large, and wise; sinewy handed, very tall, very strong; with the mouth of a bloodhound and the jaws of a bulldog". This corresponds more nearly to a description of the late Marie Dressler than of Flora Robson! But having met the actress, and seen stills of her costume and make-up, Shaw's references to her in the new scene in Cleopatra's Bedchamber seem to be modified by the impression she has made.

"Ftatateeta enters. She presents a figure different from that of the night before. She has not put on her official robe; and her powerful and handsome body is seen apparently naked except for a rich sash or sumptuous belt which serves also as an apron. (Her hair must not be woolly; she is an Egyptian slave, not an Ethiopian one: dark red brown, but not black.) Her attitude is as commanding as ever."

She is at her best in the scenes that bring her closest to Vivien Leigh, to whom she acts as a magnificent contrast and foil.

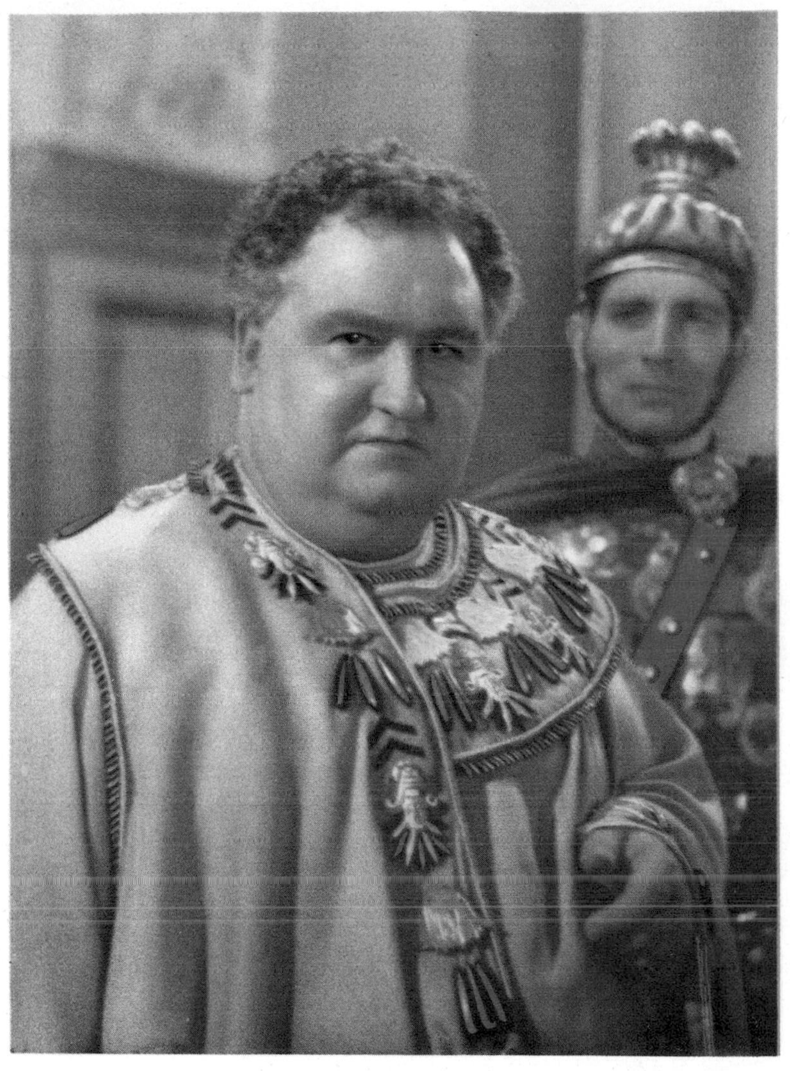

POTHINUS, THE EGYPTIAN, SEEKS AUDIENCE WITH CAESAR, AND IS ADMITTED BY THE CAPTAIN OF THE ROMAN GUARD

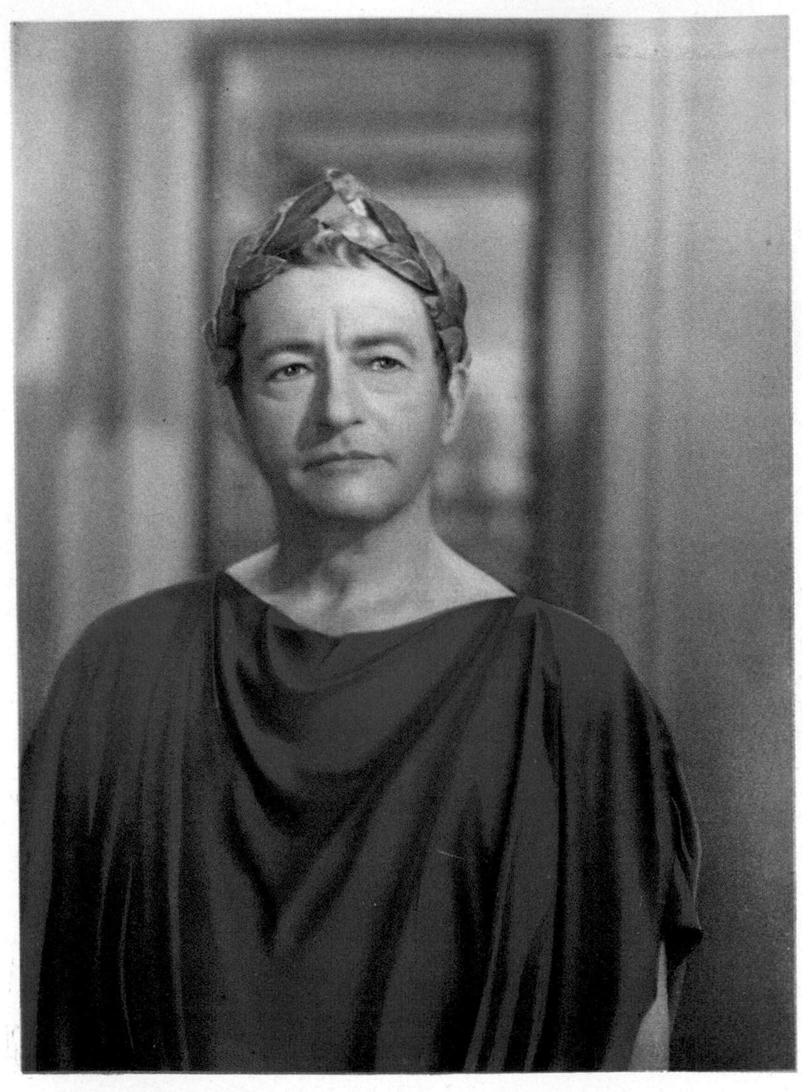

CAESAR IN THE KING'S ROOM OF THE PALACE OF ALEXANDRIA

THE BOY KING PTOLEMY, IN THE COUNCIL CHAMBER AT ALEXANDRIA

CAESAR ASSURES CLEOPATRA THAT HE WILL BE BACK SOON FROM THE

Lucius Septimius is played by Raymond Lovell, with an air and appearance that is oddly reminiscent of Jannings. The two sudden and quite unexpected appearances of Lucius Septimius are liable to perplex all but the most erudite members of the audience, as it is scarcely possible, within the scope of either play or film, to explain the exact significance of this politico-military Roman figure in the ranks of Caesar's Egyptian adversaries. He must, therefore, make an impression that is in itself ominous and arresting, so that what may be missed intellectually may be visually and emotionally supplied. The presentation of Septimius as—to quote Shaw's play once more—"a clean-shaven, trim athlete of about forty, with symmetrical features, resolute mouth, and handsome, thin Roman nose, in the dress of a Roman officer" might have given him, for film purposes, too close a resemblance to the military figure of Caesar himself. Lovell's portrayal of the character is as unorthodox as it is interesting.

No one, I think, will quarrel with the playing of *Pothinus* by Francis Sullivan. This is another of the truly Shavian portraits of the film. Like Shaw a wit and an Irishman, Sullivan has the physical languor combined with mental passion and agility of the exceptionally brilliant, adipose men of every generation who, from Falstaff to G. K. Chesterton, constitute what is almost a separate race. The gargantuan stature of his Pothinus, clad in the classical white draperies of the Greek-Egyptian aristocracy, towers over the people and politics of Alexandria just as Shaw—and, incidentally, history—destined him to do. In the final scene, where his passionate, uncontrollable temper betrays him into accusing the Queen to her face of disloyalty to Caesar, one

can almost feel the indignant, hurried pounding of his blood, the blank resentment with which he discovers that he has failed to communicate this indignation to Caesar, his immense patriotic scorn for Cleopatra, the Egyptian "with a Roman heart". And when his stabbed body falls into the courtyard, one can believe that the Egyptian mob will mourn and seek to revenge him as a hero. This is a Pothinus which is immense not merely in stature but in moral force and emotion.

Beside Pothinus in the Palace Council Chamber stands *Ptolemy*, played by young Anthony Harvey, a newcomer, not merely to the screen, but to the whole acting profession. He gives an appealing and sensitive performance in this very difficult juvenile rôle, although he is unfortunately, in my opinion, already too old and too *tall* for the part, so that the sudden mature dignities of a royal child fail of their full effect. Ptolemy, as described by Shaw, should have the precocity of some mediaeval portrait of a baby prince, overdressed and adult, yet clutching forlornly at a toy. A child young and small enough to convey this impression, yet capable of meeting the demands of a part sufficiently subtle and exacting to tax most adult actors, would be not simply an acting phenomenon and correspondingly hard to find, but would have his professional activities so severely controlled by the laws which govern the work of child-actors as to make it well-nigh impossible to include him in such big acting scenes as the ones in which Ptolemy appears.

Tony Harvey (who grew rapidly in the months which passed between the making of his screen-test and his actual appearance in the picture!) does his best—and a very good best—with the drawbacks of the situation, and his unusually large, beautiful eyes give his scenes a pathos of their own. He is not, I think, the perfect Ptolemy, but he has gifts which the screen may well show more of in the future.

Almost last, but very far from least, in my alphabetical list of principals comes Basil Sydney's *Rufio*, another of Gabriel Pascal's against-type casting triumphs. Sydney has always been regarded as an emotional, romantic actor, figuring mainly in "lover" rôles: for years he played opposite Doris Keane in *Romance*, and is more recently remembered as the title-player in *Love From a Stranger*. His transformation into the bluff, terse, "no-nonsense" type of warrior, Caesar's loyal but often exasperated comrade-at-arms, is startling in its authenticity and vigour. At every point of his appearance in the film, he has the keen, preoccupied air of a soldier whose mind is busy dealing with its strategic and military problems. The hundred-and-one other considerations which engage Caesar's attention—women, politics, points of manners and morals and ethics—seem to Rufio a frivolous waste of time, and his fundamental impatience with them is constantly at war with his boundless admiration for his General. It is the kind of admiration which only a truly simple and warm-hearted man can feel for one who is his intellectual superior; and it is the manner in which he conveys this simplicity, this fundamental *goodness* of a ruthless man of action, which makes Sydney's performance a genuine masterpiece.

Partly because many of their scenes were shared, partly because of their long-standing professional friendship, Basil Sydney and Cecil Parker were constantly to be seen in one another's company during the making of the picture. Their characterisations grew together and reacted on one another, and a bond of genuine behind-the-camera comradeship seems to me to have woven itself into the texture of the film. Their team-playing is one of its dominating factors.

Finally, the *Theodotus* of Ernest Thesiger: there is no need to enlarge upon this otherwise than by saying that, in the crafty, officious, passionately intellectual scholar who is the boy-king's tutor, Thesiger has a Shavian part peculiarly suited to his peculiar histrionic abilities. One accepts him instantly as the character he portrays, savouring its nature in the malice and opportunism of the Council Chamber sequence no less than in the sincerity of his frantic despair over the burning of the famous Library. It is not, frankly, one of my favourite rôles in the play, being one of the very rare cases where I feel Shaw has been content to create what is more or less a "stock" character, without the addition of any of those warmly-inspired human touches in which resides the generosity of his genius. But given the faint chill of Theodotus, one can enjoy watching it played by such an artist as Thesiger, whose diction, movements, and strange, finely-cut features are always a pleasure to see.

Those are the acting principals in *Caesar and Cleopatra*, and the list omits an unprecedented number of brilliant front-rank players who subscribed to Pascal's fanatic conviction that for any and every Shaw part, be it the solitary line of a market-place bystander or Palace attendant, or even the silent reaction of a slave, none but the best obtainable acting talent will do. The picture is memorable for a score of performances which might be termed "minor" were they not so unmistakably first-class. To mention a few of them, there is the stalwart, laughing Belzanor of Stanley Holloway; Alan Wheatley's insinuating Persian (whose costume is, incidentally, a triumph of Messel's art); the challenging, swaggering Bel Affris of Leo Genn; Robert Adams, the coloured artist who is making a great name for himself in British films and the theatre, as Cleopatra's Nubian slave; Michael Rennie's fine Captain of the Guard; John Bryning's truculent sentinel; Antony Holles, Charles Victor and Ronald Shiner as a trio of Alexandrian ruffians, turning their hands to whatever money-making, casual employment the city might offer, and supplying an Egyptian chorus to the dramatic and political issues of the story. There is Olga Edwardes' impertinent, lovely Charmian; little Jean Simmonds' harpist; Don Kenito's street singer; the mannered, exquisite Major Domo of Esmé Percy. There is young Abdul Wahab, whom Pascal saw one day walking quietly along a London street and promptly press-ganged into the film as Cleopatra's personal boy-attendant. There is a camel-driver, played by Gabriel Pascal himself, because only he understood and was understood by the camel, and could make it do what he wanted. And there is the camel, who bit Gabriel Pascal . . .

Honour is due, too, to the crowd. In all, nearly two thousand film extras were used in the big mob and battle scenes of the picture, and their acting co-operation was so responsive and enthusiastic that they have made a genuine contribution to the spirit of the story. Pascal makes great demands on his crowd artists. To him, they are never just a crowd, however large, but a group of individuals, each one of whom must give a satisfactory human and dramatic performance. His way of suddenly interrupting a scene involving hundreds of people, to reproach some almost invisible unit for not playing his or her full part in the proceedings, is apt to be regarded as a somewhat obstructive form of directorial eccentricity; but the result is that the people he is directing come to regard themselves as essential factors in the drama, and so to throw themselves into it with a spirit and abandon seldom achieved in picture-making—certainly not in British picture-making, where our inherent national traits of reserve and shyness have to be overcome before the performers can do the best of which they are capable.

In his work on these scenes Pascal received invaluable help from his Australian assistant-director, Bluey Hill, whose good-natured and often very witty microphone handling of the players also did much to secure their willing co-operation.

Finally, to the many gifted artists whose names I have omitted from this chapter through lack of space but not of appreciation, my apologies, and Gabriel Pascal's thanks.

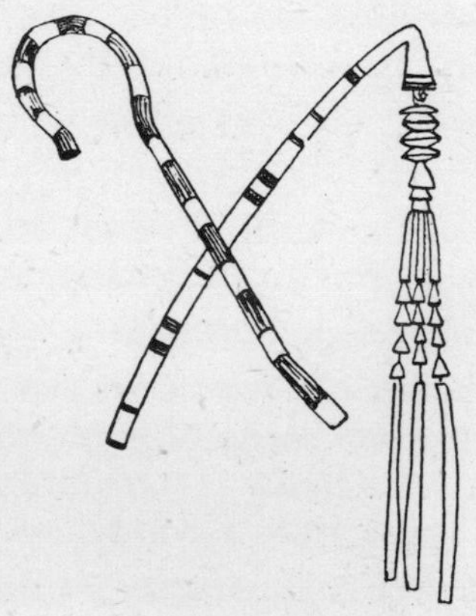

PRODUCTION DIFFICULTIES

GABRIEL PASCAL started shooting *Caesar and Cleopatra* on June 12th, 1944, just six days after D-Day.

Our first set—the Sphinx—had given everybody concerned a great deal of trouble before it was ready. (Its nose, I seem to remember, had to be remodelled by Pascal personally, swinging beside it in a painter's cradle, before he was satisfied with the result!) And it continued to give trouble during the first few days of shooting. The scenes between Vivien Leigh and Claude Rains sitting vis-à-vis on its huge paws had to be shot on a level with the action from high camera rostrums, and these had constantly to be moved and re-erected in accordance with the movements of the players. It would have been simple enough with an up-to-date camera crane, but the only available apparatus was not suited to the much increased weight and bulk of the Technicolor camera, and it was impossible to obtain or manufacture a new crane in wartime.

On the Thursday night after our fourth day of shooting, London had a peculiar and very unpleasant air-raid, and the following day we learnt that we had had our first experience of the new flying-bombs or "pilotless planes", as we used at that time to call them. Two days later Gabriel Pascal and nine or ten members of his unit, myself among them, had a narrow escape from death when, while we were inspecting the outdoor Pharos set, then in course of construction on top of a thirty-foot-high rostrum in the studio grounds, a sudden outburst of ack-ack gunfire almost directly overhead drew our attention to a small black object like a model aeroplane descending straight and rapidly towards us; and how we managed to get down from that platform in time to fling ourselves to the ground before the explosion made it heave and shake under us is something I shall never quite remember or understand.

This form of air-attack, while it never again came quite so close to the studio itself, grew steadily worse during the first six or eight weeks of shooting, and had a disastrous effect on the progress of the production, which it impeded and slowed up in every kind of direct and indirect way. Not only were transport and postal and telephone communications interfered with, so that everything was behindhand, and actors and staff alike had difficulty in getting to and from the studio, but nobody could get much sleep, and the simplest problems seemed to become insuperable. One or two members of the cast and unit suffered actual loss. Many more, if not most, had hurriedly to reorganise their own and their families' domestic lives.

Less grave, but even more continuously disintegrating, were the indirect effects of this form of enemy action. Shops and supply-depôts were closed, and materials arrived weeks after the orders had been given. Most badly hit of all, perhaps, were the dressmaking workrooms where our two-thousand-odd specially designed costumes were in process of being made. These workrooms were staffed very largely by young girls of fourteen and upwards, under the call-up age; and their mothers, evacuating from the danger-area with the younger members of the family, were naturally unwilling to leave such juvenile daughters behind. Almost the whole of this essential dressmaking population disappeared from the London workrooms during the first week or two of the flying-bomb raids, and the costumes had to be turned out somehow by the proprietors themselves, aided by a few harassed, overworked but indefatigable older members of their staffs.

Apart from these flying-bomb drawbacks, we were handicapped from the outset of production in other ways. The shortage of skilled craftsmen was making itself felt,

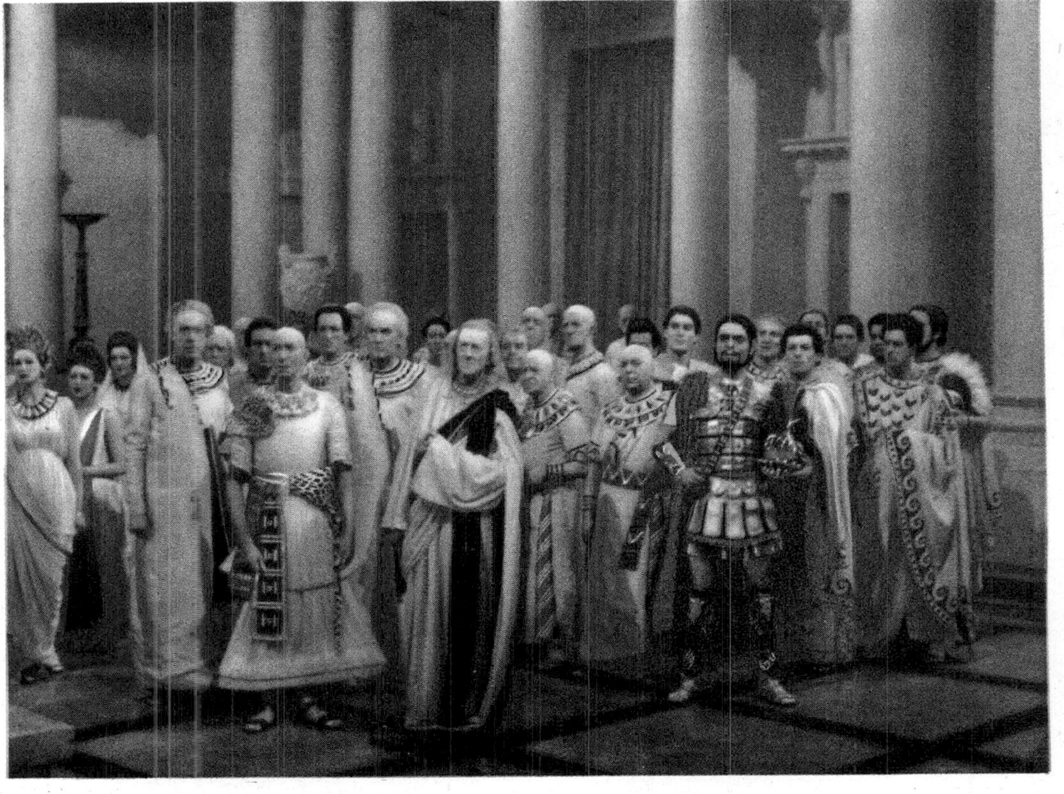

A GROUP OF EGYPTIAN GOVERNMENT OFFICIALS IN THE COUNCIL CHAMBER AT ALEXANDRIA

CLEOPATRA RESTING IN HER MUSIC ROOM

by this stage of the war, in every branch of the film industry, and most of all among the plasterers, whose work is the indispensable basis of modern film-set construction. We started the production needing at least fifty additional plasterers if we were to keep our gigantic building programme up to schedule; and our failure to do so was at any rate partly due to the fact that these additional highly-skilled men were flatly unobtainable.

Perhaps the worst of all our production-hindrances was the weather! A big spectacular picture like *Caesar and Cleopatra* cannot be made indoors; and we seldom had a worse summer than that of 1944, unless it was the summer of 1945, when, in order to repair the previous year's deficiencies, Pascal built an enormous location-set reproducing parts of the city of Alexandria, and spent week after week, and month after month out there, waiting for the sun. In the end, we got all the essential scenes, but the process was heartbreaking; and without the unfailing resourcefulness and persistence of Tom White, Denham's General Manager of Production, who always had a cheerful solution for what seemed insoluble till he appeared, the picture could scarcely have survived its non-stop series of crises.

These wartime and weather obstacles were augmented by one or two quite unforeseeable catastrophes which hit us midway through production, while we were working on the big Palace Roof set, which supplies the background for Cleopatra's banquet, given in Caesar's honour, and its highly dramatic sequel. Halfway through this key-scene—just at the point, indeed, where the Queen leads her guests to the lavishly-appointed dinner-table—Vivien Leigh was taken ill, and we were held up for a matter of from five to six weeks all told. The alternative exterior shooting which might have relieved the situation was once again dependent on the worst possible weather-conditions; and the fact that Claude Rains' contract had been entered into on the positive understanding that he would be free to return to America about the middle of October, and that, if this condition were not observed, the Rank organisation would become liable for thousands of pounds of Income Tax on his behalf, added a touch of hopelessness to the general sense of *impasse* which had by now reduced the unit's working morale to a point only a little above zero.

That the picture was *not* abandoned at this critical juncture is due solely to the faith and determination of two people: Arthur Rank and Gabriel Pascal. Both have been bitterly criticised in the press and in the inner and outer circles of the film-industry for embarking on and persisting in such a colossal venture at such a difficult time, and I think it is possible that the general public, who have not, for the most part, joined in the chorus of condemnation, may like to hear what is to be said on the other side of this one-sided discussion. Arthur Rank believed that, for the establishment and survival of the British film-industry in the post-war period of hectic international trade competition, it was essential to have ready a few really first-class super-productions aimed, not merely at our own, but at the world-market. He did not think, in spite of the limited studio space at our disposal, the scarcity of first-rate technicians, the shortage of skilled labour and materials, that the preparation of such pictures could be delayed until the war was over and the industrial situation back to normal or capable of being expanded. He considered—and I think rightly—that the immediate post-war situation was vital, and that unless we had something to offer over and above the less expensive, often highly interesting pictures intended primarily for the home market, we should be liable to lose our place altogether as a force to be reckoned with in international picture-making.

This is certainly no excuse for squandering money unnecessarily on any picture, however lavish its design. But it is fair to say that, once embarked on a production of the magnitude of a *Caesar and Cleopatra*, it is impossible to foresee with exactitude the total expense involved, especially at such a time of danger and difficulty as the year 1944–45.

Gabriel Pascal's desire to keep on with the production in spite of every drawback was naturally inspired not so much by this long-term policy as by his wish to produce the major Shaw subjects in the author's lifetime, and this particular one first of all, because of the brilliant star-asset of Vivien Leigh, who could not be indefinitely available for the part of Cleopatra. Once embarked on it, I think he would have continued to make it, if necessary, in a fathoms-deep underground shelter, under a rain of atomic bombs! He and Rank were, at all events, united in their determination to finish the picture at all costs, and Claude Rains' departure date was postponed until December.

After he left we had to complete a number of sets in which Caesar did not appear, among them Cleopatra's Music Room in which she passes the time with her ladies; and this particular set presented us with a new outcrop of wartime production problems. It was very attractive, with an artificial pool in the centre, and windows and archways opening along one side on to a formal garden with lawns and flowering trees. Pascal had set his heart on obtaining some white peacocks to adorn this garden, and it was a great disappointment to him when the only ones that could be found were not allowed by their owners to travel into the London area, which was now menaced by rockets as well as flying-bombs, so that we had to make do with the ordinary coloured variety, although these looked sufficiently decorative to me. As for the bevy of lovely girls who were to recline around the pool, they were almost as hard to come by as white peacocks, because at this time the Flower of English Girlhood was most stringently controlled by National Service Regulations, and the Production Manager was harassed by despairing visits and telephone messages from Venus-like creatures who had been "directed" to factories in the North of England in the middle of having their costumes fitted. However, in this case persistence triumphed, and we managed to hold on to our quota of loveliness just long enough to finish shooting the Music Room scenes before the factories and Services snatched it away.

By the beginning of February, 1945, Vivien Leigh's part in the picture was finished, and all the essential interior scenes were complete. For some time past the great "To Be or Not To Be" of the production had centred round the question of an Egyptian location. Were actual Egyptian exteriors needed to perfect the picture? Pascal was craving for the great open spaces of an actual desert, the blueness of a Mediterranean sky, to release the film from its Denham confinement, and in this instinctive inclination he was supported by a predominantly male element among his associates, once again headed by Arthur Rank, who felt that British pictures were often handicapped by a faintly claustrophobic indoor quality as the result of our climate, and that, if the Government considered Egypt practicable, it should not be denied to the production.

There was at this time an inevitable come-and-go of transport between this country and the Mediterranean of such frequency and volume that the requirements of a solitary film-location made an inconsiderable addition to its bulk. We were given the dates of various cargo sailings, our costumes and properties—including the Sphinx, in its several sections—were crated and sent down to the docks, various members of the essential unit went ahead to make advance investigations and arrangements, and the remainder, including Pascal himself, followed as soon as everything was ready.

CLEOPATRA TRIES TO BRIBE THE GUARD TO ALLOW HER OUT OF THE PALACE

THEODOTUS BRINGS NEWS OF THE BURNING LIBRARY TO CAESAR

Much to my regret, though with the fullest recognition of my non-essential quality on such an expedition, I did not go to Egypt, so the information that follows was supplied by Raymond Anzarut, Pascal's Egyptian Location Manager, who gave invaluable assistance throughout the undertaking.

The Sphinx was assembled and set up in the desert at Beni Ussef, a location outside Cairo; and the maiden shot of the expedition was that of Caesar and Cleopatra walking back hand-in-hand from the Sphinx towards her "Palace in the Desert". It seemed that the unit had brought the English weather with them, for as soon as they tried to make the shot it started to rain in Cairo, where rain is almost unknown, and the scene was finally made in bitter cold at six-thirty in the morning.

Two aero-engines and a crew of six R.A.F. men were used to produce the sandstorm around the Sphinx. Once again the weather kept the unit waiting—this time for a real sandstorm to die down before the artificial one could begin!

This business of preferring controllable artifice to uncontrollable nature is something that never fails to disconcert and astonish the uninitiated in film-making. Why not shoot the real sandstorm? they ask, not only amazed but definitely resentful, feeling they have been cheated of reality yet again. The answer is that the real sandstorm would produce a choking blur on the screen, through which the objects to be photographed would be quite simply invisible.

In the same way, the most frequent question put to the unit by people in Egypt was: "Why did you have to bring your own Sphinx out here, when the original is still standing?"

The answer to this was, in the first place, that the Sphinx where Cleopatra and Caesar met was never intended to be the Great Sphinx, but a quite different and much smaller member of the same species. "This isn't the Great Sphinx," Cleopatra tells Caesar. "This is only a dear little kitten of the Sphinx." Moreover, our two characters on the actual Sphinx would have been so far apart as to make any thought of conversation between them entirely out of the question, so that, even had we decided to disregard the fact that twenty centuries of wear and tear must be supposed to have altered the Egyptian Sphinx considerably since Cleopatra's day, we could not possibly have used it for the purposes of our scene.

It is understandable that technical considerations of this sort should not occur to ordinary members of the public, to whom the idea of taking a Sphinx to Egypt seems almost as odd and unnecessary as the proverbial business of carrying coals to Newcastle; but I have been astonished by the ignorance displayed by serious British film-critics and journalists, who are supposed to understand at least the A B C of film-technique, and in whom the naïveté of imagining that our studio Sphinx scenes could be matched with others taken around the Great Sphinx itself is really inexcusable.

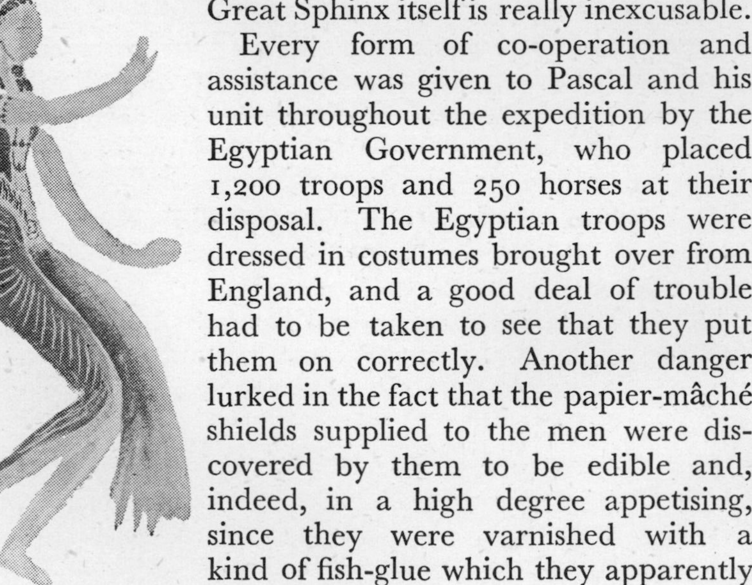

Every form of co-operation and assistance was given to Pascal and his unit throughout the expedition by the Egyptian Government, who placed 1,200 troops and 250 horses at their disposal. The Egyptian troops were dressed in costumes brought over from England, and a good deal of trouble had to be taken to see that they put them on correctly. Another danger lurked in the fact that the papier-mâché shields supplied to the men were discovered by them to be edible and, indeed, in a high degree appetising, since they were varnished with a kind of fish-glue which they apparently liked very much. Three hundred new shields had to be made in Egypt to supply the deficiencies caused by this outbreak of shield consumption.

Scenes in the picture which were actually taken in Egypt include long shots around the Sphinx, the Roman legions marching through the desert to Alexandria, battle scenes in the desert, shots of Alexandria harbour and the Pharos lighthouse, and Caesar's homeward-bound galley setting sail across the Mediterranean. There is also a very beautiful shot, leading into the battle scenes, of Roman troops marching alongside a rose-tinted lake, suggesting the reflection of a sky at sunrise. This is the salt lake of Edku, some eighty-five miles from Alexandria, and its water is actually tinged with pink, due to a mysterious combination of certain chemicals with the salt deposits. As soon as he saw it, Gaby set his heart on a scene shot across this lake; but when all arrangements had been made and the unit arrived on the scene with their equipment, the lake was found to be bone dry, and local farmers assured them that it would not fill up again before the following winter. Pascal himself had by this time left Egypt, and cables kept on arriving from him urging the absolute necessity of a shot across the pink lake. The desperate unit, anxious to get home themselves, were starting to discuss ways and means of filling the lake artificially when one day a miraculous tide occurred, and they just had time before it dried up again to get the shot organized, racing the thirsty sun to get one of the most beautiful scenes in the picture.

To save return transport the Denham Sphinx was left behind in the desert, where I am told it now rivals its ancient prototype as a photographic background for tourists.

THE MUSIC

"For this film we need a French music!" Pascal announced triumphantly.

The problem of the music had been worrying him all through the making of the picture. He had approached both Benjamin Britten and William Walton, for whose work he has the greatest admiration, but neither of them were at the time free to take on such a prolonged work of composition; nor was Prokoviev, his idol among contemporary Russian composers, able to come over here for the purpose. But once the idea of "a French music" had taken hold of him, no other kind would do. English music would be too reflective, too religious in its origins, Russian music, for all its orientalism, too barbaric and sensual for the slightly acid, always *fresh* quality of Bernard Shaw's play. Only a French composer would know how to stylise its Eastern atmosphere, at the same time contriving to accentuate its mannered Western wit. "A French music" it had to be.

Georges Auric, one of the famous "Les Six" group of modern French musicians, has had considerable experience as a composer of film-music, and, still more of composing for the ballet, with which the technique of film-composition has a great deal in common. Besides *Caesar and Cleopatra*, London has recently heard his work in Michael Balcon's *Dead of Night*, and the first of our batch of French films, *L'éternel Retour*.

A big, loosely-built, rather indolent-looking man, Auric composes with an absent air, sitting humped up over the piano with a cigarette dangling from his lips, under frowning, half-closed eyes, and plays his own melodies apologetically—"Je ne suis pas pianist, vous savez!"—with

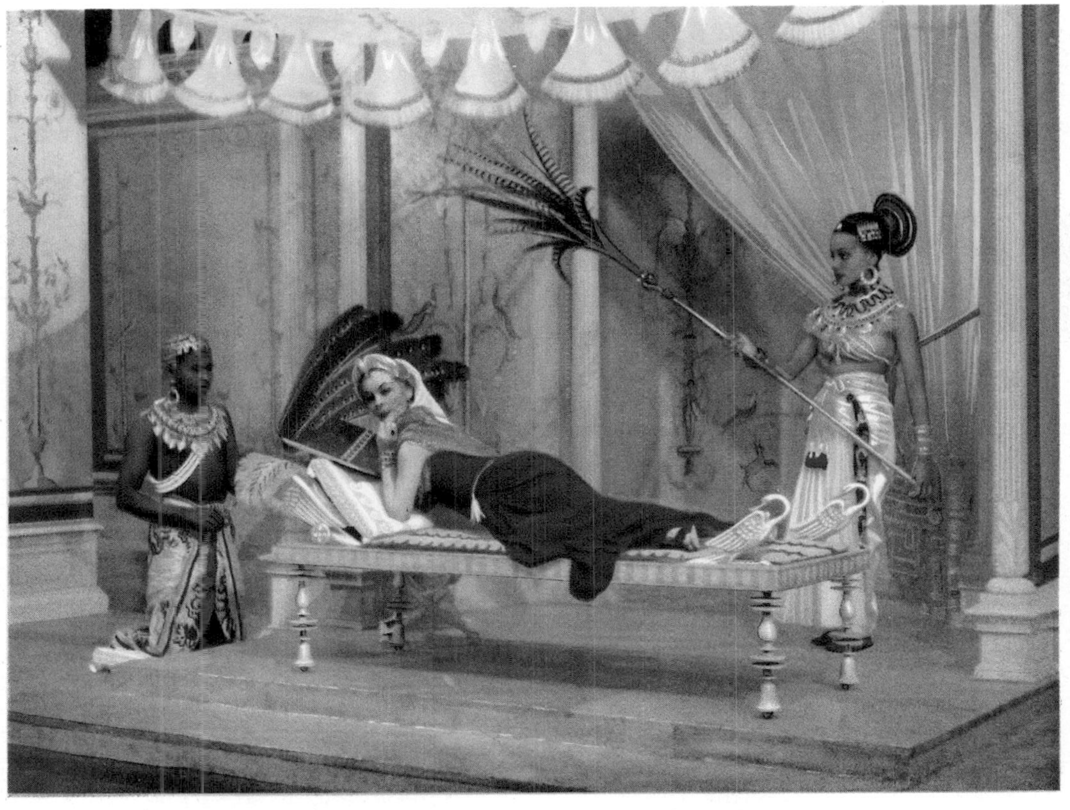

CLEOPATRA, WITH HER ATTENDANTS IN THE MUSIC ROOM

CLEOPATRA AND CAESAR IN THE COUNCIL CHAMBER OF ALEXANDRIA

ACHILLAS, THE EGYPTIAN GENERAL, IN THE COUNCIL CHAMBER

THE YOUNG HARPIST ENTERTAINS THE QUEEN AND HER LADIES-IN-WAITING

hands that look curiously large and inexpert on the keys. Can he really do this film-job, one wonders? Can he compose with the precision and accuracy demanded by this most exacting musical medium? He looks too relaxed and easy-going to be capable of so much strain and concentration.

But he takes it all so easily, it presently appears, because it is so easy for him. So many feet of film, so many bars of music—"Bien, bien! Entendu!" He nods his head, and smokes, and strums a little; and very soon there it all is, graceful and effortless, the Cleopatra motif, the Caesarean theme, weaving in and out of the lovely, dreaming music of the Sphinx, the battle-music of the Roman legions, the young Queen's lullaby, the languorous background of the royal banquet, till finally, with the urgent swell and beat of newly-spread sails, it carries Caesar's galley away from Egypt on its journey back to Rome.

"When that boat sails away," said Bernard Shaw, the music-critic, "Auric's music touches greatness. It is almost Handelian."

Coming from G.B.S., there could scarcely be higher praise. Handel is one of his gods.

The music was recorded by the National Symphony Orchestra, conducted by Muir Mathieson. Shaw was present at one of their sessions, and Gabriel Pascal took an active part in all of them, sitting with the recording-staff in the sound-booth, and darting out on to the balcony outside after every rehearsal to harangue the musicians, who found his comments unorthodox but stimulating.

The result is an unusually apt performance of a lovely film-symphony, providing to my mind the perfect aural background to the picture.

THE COSTUMES AND DECOR

It is an old and rather irritating adage that Necessity is the Mother of Invention: but it happens time and again that an artist, encountering obstacles and difficulties in the performance of his work, has been forced to employ makeshift expedients which have actually resulted in a heightening of artistic achievement.

Caesar and Cleopatra in Technicolor, with Vivien Leigh as Cleopatra, sounds like every dress-designer's dream assignment. The dearth of fabrics and decorative materials, and the appalling shortage of workroom staff, must have transformed the dream into something more like an actual nightmare for Oliver Messel; but in spite of every deprivation and drawback, his costumes and decor somehow achieved the gossamer dreamlike quality of an Egyptian fairy-tale.

His military experience as an officer in charge of a camouflage unit stood him in good stead. Since nothing he wanted for his designs was ever remotely obtainable, he had to make whatever he could get look quite unlike itself, which is the essence of camouflage. Authentic antique Egyptian jewellery was copied in thin wire, plastics, cellophane, bits of glass—anything Messel and his talented staff of assistants could lay their hands on. Gold plates and table ornaments were made from a combination of gilded leather and papier mâché. The oriental department at a London store was ransacked, and the most striking costumes were contrived out of Indian *saris*, or hangings and cotton bedspreads printed in excellent hand-blocked Egyptian and Persian designs. Curtains of coupon-free gauze were stencilled with authentic patterns of the period in specially mixed dyes. Messel's assistant, Elinor Abbey, toiled for days and nights over the countless jewels of Cleopatra's coronation robe, sewing them on, one by one, by hand. He himself often sat up all night working on the intricate details of a head-dress or necklet; and was to be seen in the daytime, pale and distraught, frantically lamenting that such-and-such an essential component of his latest masterpiece of decor would not be ready in time, and the whole effect would be ruined. But such tragedies were always circumvented at the last moment by some triumph of contrivance, and the resulting presentation was complete.

The detail of every costume and every piece of decoration is noteworthy. Notice the fringed bed-hangings in Cleopatra's bedroom, her head-dress in the Banqueting sequence, the embossed designs on the Roman shields (see p. 27), the collars on the Court-Ladies' dresses, the feather fans in the lovely Music Room where the girl harpist plays, and the flail and crook carried by Cleopatra at her coronation (p. 88). All these had to be specially designed and made for the picture, and every last bird and bead and arabesque is the outcome of meticulous research combined with Messel's individual artistry.

His team of artist experts were adept as interpreters of his creative intentions: Matilda Etches in carrying out the brilliant costume designs from his sketches, a few of which, much reduced in size and robbed of the colour which is an essential part of the artist's conception, are nevertheless effectively reproduced in the margins of this book; Elinor Abbey and Maggie Furse in the wardrobe; Arthur Boys in furnishing and property details; Hugh Skillan in special head-dresses; Scott-Slymon in stencilling and dyeing; Beatrice Dawson in hand-made jewellery and accessories; Raoh Schorr in sculpture. All these contributed with great talent and devotion to the final harmony of colour, texture and form.

The results enter into the spirit of Pascal's production in a remarkable way. The visual detail of the picture has become involved with its sense, so that, in thinking of certain scenes, their colours and designs stand out in the imagination like dramatic symbols. Although rarely achieved, that is, or should be, the aim of film and theatrical design. It is the token of genuine artistry; and I think that Oliver Messel's reputation as an artist will be greatly affirmed and enhanced by his work on this production.

THE SETS

THE sets for *Caesar and Cleopatra*, including several of the finest and most elaborate ever constructed for a British picture, were designed by John Bryan, the young Art Director of Gainsborough Pictures, who, because he had already worked on both the previous Shaw-Pascal films, *Pygmalion* and *Major Barbara*, was loaned to the new production at Pascal's special request.

It was a tremendous task, and John Bryan is one of the very few men in the British industry whose artistry as a designer is backed by the technical knowledge and experience necessary to express it in terms of classic architecture and practical construction. "Art Director" has always seemed to me a rather vague classification of what should, I think, be more aptly termed "Film Architect", at all events on a production of this scope; and I note with interest that one of the leading engineering colleges in London now includes a course on Film Architecture in its curriculum. Any structural expert will realise that sets of the magnitude and classic proportions of those shown in *Caesar and Cleopatra* must be designed, not simply by an artist, but by one who is a trained architect as well. It is no use designing vast pillars and archways and terraces to be carried out in a lath-and-plaster imitation of solid wood and stone unless the principles governing actual structure in the imitated materials are adhered to. The work of a scenic designer, particularly on a film which combines early Egyptian architecture with that of Greece in the first century B.C., is largely one of visual balance, combining height, size and *apparent* weight in faithful proportions, based on an intimate knowledge of the styles, forms and types of material originally employed.

The ancient Memphis Palace, to which Cleopatra brings Caesar after their encounter at the Sphinx, is the largest interior set in the picture. It occupied over 28,000 square feet of floor space, and each of its pseudo-granite columns, carved from base to crown with authentic Egyptian figures and hieroglyphs, measured nineteen feet in diameter and weighed a couple of tons. The great stone gods, including the "vast marble cats, and figures of men with hawk's heads" of Shaw's description, which stand between the pillars, are all faithfully reproduced from Egyptian originals. The effect is one of awe-inspiring size and grandeur, so that the living figures of Caesar and Cleopatra, making their entrance through the deserted collonade, are dwarfed, not into insignificance, but strangely enough into exactly the opposite, so that we see them momentarily as pygmies actuated by a curious purpose and power.

The next great interior set of the picture, King Ptolemy's Council Chamber, has a very different appearance from the ancient palace of his ancestors, and thus supplies a visual comment on the change that had come over the Egyptian monarchy through the centuries. The architecture of the modern palace at Alexandria has not even an echo of the savage native force of the country and the people it dominates. It is purely imitative, the graceful springing pillars and archways of neo-Grecian architecture giving an impression of light and airiness as far as possible removed from the dim barbaric grandeurs of Memphis.

At the far end of the Council Chamber double doors opened into the King's Room, presently to be taken over by Caesar as his office and military headquarters; and facing these doors a wide balconied window was made to overlook the city and harbour of Alexandria, which had to be entirely constructed in miniature, quite the loveliest and most convincing of its kind I have ever seen.

An unusual number of these miniatures were employed in the film, sometimes as a complete effect, as in the case of this view from the King's Room window, sometimes in trick shots, where the actual set photographed stopped short at a certain height from the ground, and the top of the screen was filled in with a miniature construction placed immediately in front of the camera, or by a superimposed painting on glass, the work of that magician of these effect shots, Percy Day. Impressions of tremendous size and distance were produced in this way at various points in the picture. It is for the audience to discover where these occur, if they are not too much caught up in the whole great spectacle and drama of the film itself to analyse the mechanics of its making!

Other notable sets in the picture are, first of all, the much-publicised, much-travelled Sphinx, 36 feet long and 27 feet high, based on a small-scale model by Raoh Schorr; the Pharos set, built out-of-doors on a 30-foot high rostrum to obtain a clear background of sky; Cleopatra's bedroom, and the Music Room where she sits with her ladies (these last two being actually more outstanding as examples of Messel's decor than of architectural design); and finally, and, perhaps, most remarkable of all, the great exterior set of the Palace Steps and Quayside, dominated by the curling prow of Caesar's galley, which provides the background for the final scene of the picture.

John Bryan was assisted in his work by the artist Heine Heckroth, and by an experienced staff of draughtsmen in the Denham Art Department; and his own technical skill and imaginative vision were reinforced by the artistic teamwork and enthusiasm, expressing itself in patient experiment and prolonged research into the history and architecture of the period, shown by everyone connected with this side of the production.

LIST OF PHOTOGRAPHIC ILLUSTRATIONS

STILLS BY WILFRED NEWTON

115

117

118

119

120

122

123

126

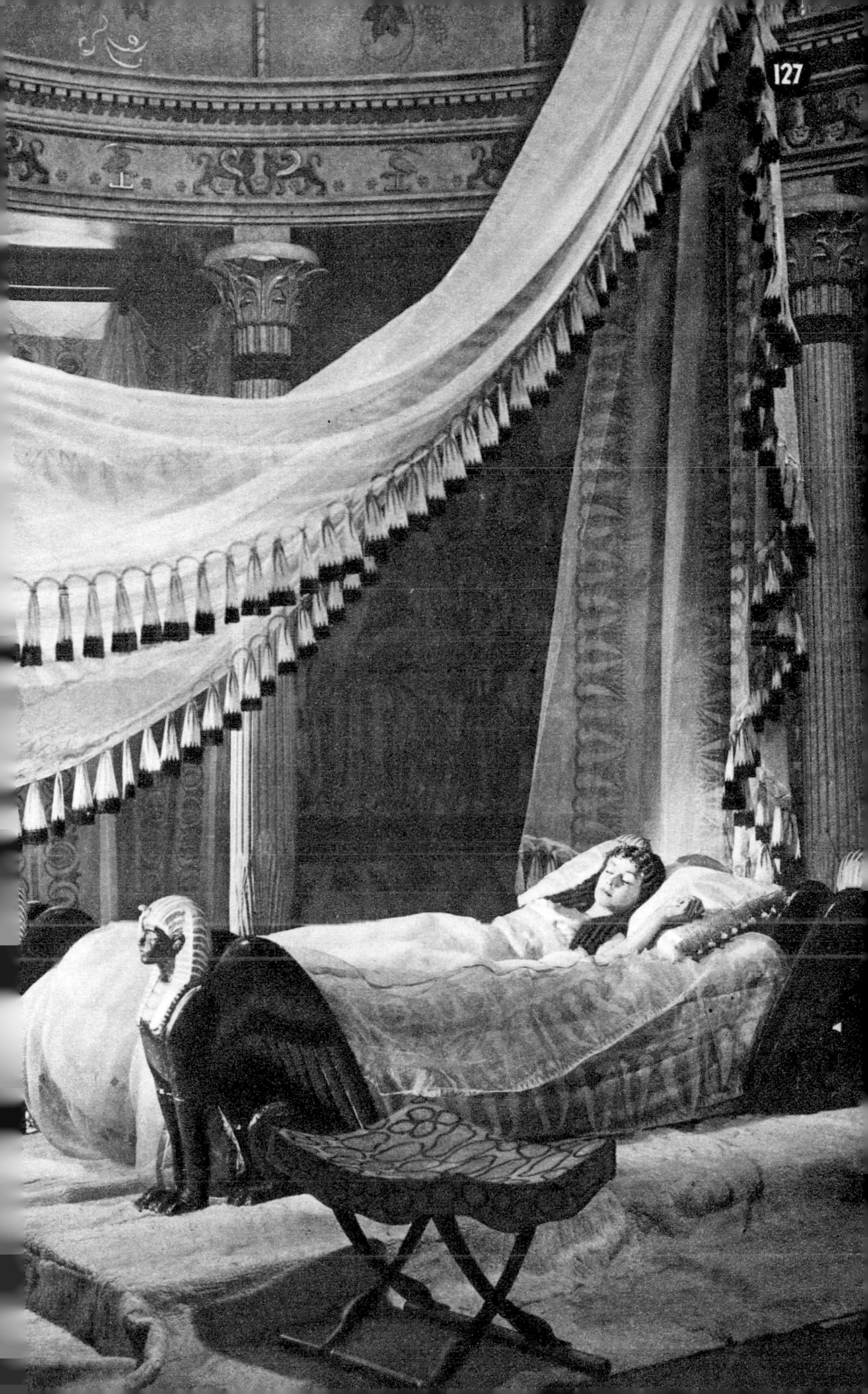

130

132

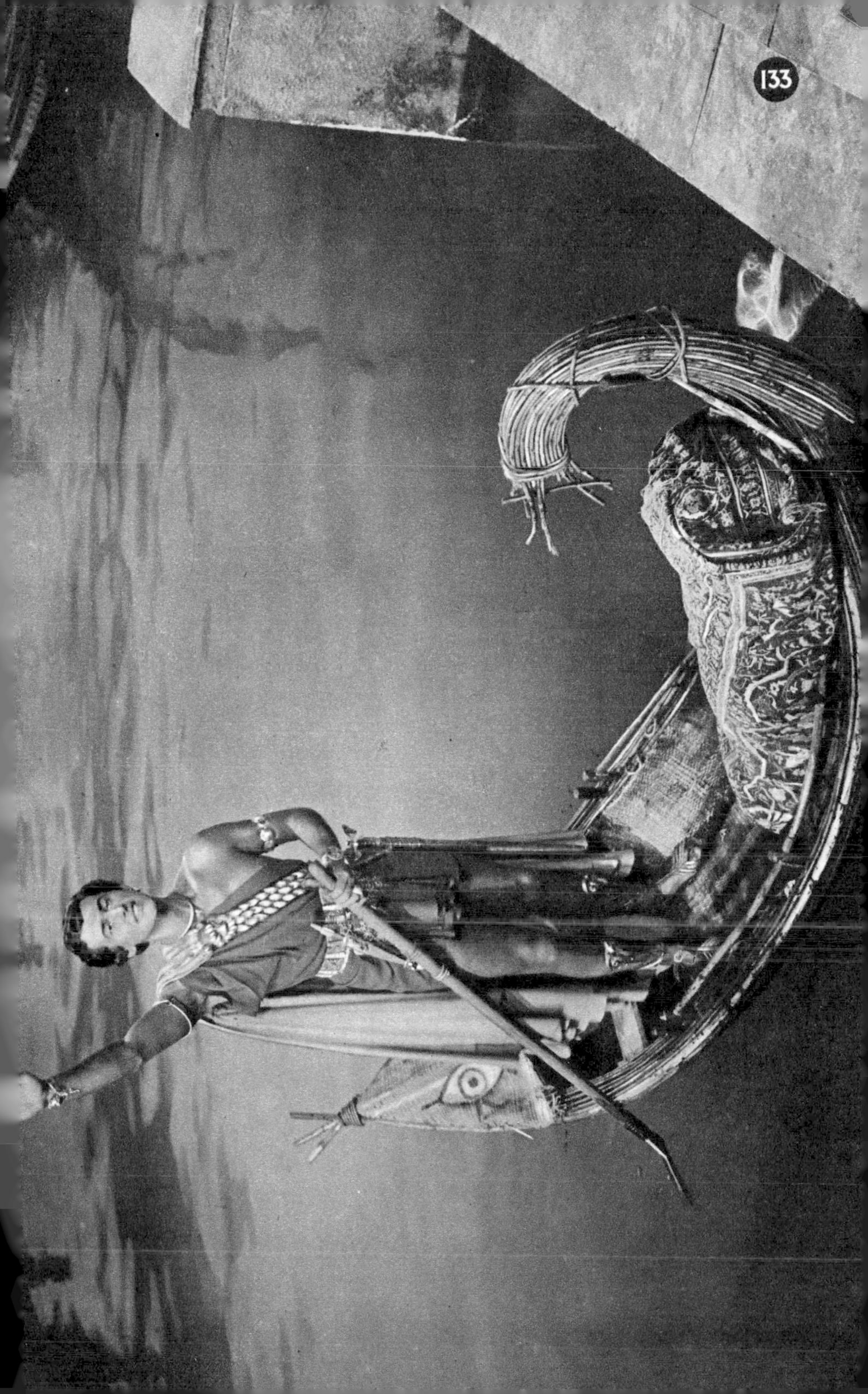

134

135

136

137

140

141

144

145